Evidence that Self-Directed Education Works

Evidence that Self-Directed Education Works

PETER GRAY

TIPPING POINTS PRESS
The Alliance for Self-Directed Education
CAMBRIDGE, MA, USA

Published by Tipping Points Press
The Alliance for Self-Directed Education

First paperback edition published in 2020 by Tipping Points Press

ISBN: 978-1-952837-02-9 (paperback)
ISBN: 978-1-952837-03-6 (ebook)

Library of Congress Cataloging-in-Publication Data
Names: Gray, Peter, author.
Title: Evidence that Self-Directed Education Works
Description: Tipping Points Press, The Alliance for Self-Directed Education
    [2020] | Includes biographical references and index.
Subjects: Alternative education, Educational research, Self-direction
    (psychology).
Identifiers: ISBN 978-1-952837-02-9 (paperback) | ISBN 978-1-952837-03-6
    (ebook)

The chapters published in this book were previously published as separate articles in Peter Gray's column, "Freedom to Learn" in *Psychology Today* and are presented here with permission.

Cover Illustration Credit: Zaki Clements
Cover & Interior Design Credit: Elliott Beard

Contents

Editor's Preface

Myriad thinkers before our time have diagnosed the ills of conventional educational systems and prescribed their cures. Dr. Peter Gray's magnificent contributions to this vital field, however, transcend the familiar routine of pointing out problems and proposing new methods to replace them. He rightly reframes the issue in the broader terms of civil liberties—in particular, the rights of children—and identifies the primary need for young people to take back their childhood. Peter has spent a remarkable 36-year career researching the relationship children have historically had with play and learning in their societies since the time of hunters and gatherers. In doing so, he has established a broad, humanitarian view of childhood that counteracts our culture's myopic, impersonal focus on assessment and workforce training. This compendium of essays, categorized by subject, catalogues the complete thoughts thus far of Dr. Gray's research on the importance of childhood freedom.

Peter's research and writing have made significant impacts on diverse populations concerned with the wellbeing and education of children, shifting his readers' thinking on children's rights and their understanding of what childhood has looked like over the history of humankind. I have heard innumerable firsthand accounts of the effect of Peter's work on parents, educators, play advocates, young people, and youth rights activists ranging from Sub-Saharan Africa to the Baltic States and from East Asia to South America. For example, a mother in Greece told me how Peter's writing motivated her to withdraw her child from the local school system and start a democratic education movement. A Sudbury school struggling to open in Turkey, where Self-Directed Education is illegal, attested to me that his writing inspired them to try it despite the risk and difficulty. A teenager in the U.S. Midwest attributed Peter's writing as the foundation of her effort to drop out of school and become an unschooler.

This begs the question, what is it about Dr. Gray's insightful research and writing that universally seems to inspire a new generation to risk breaking with convention and to actualize freedom through education, parenting, and personal growth? I cannot speak for all, but I think I may have an inkling. Peter's experience as a research professor of evolutionary, developmental, and educational psychology gives him an advantageous perspective on the subject of child rearing and learning. He is able to draw his readers out of society's normative obsession with assessment and workforce productivity, and compel us to pursue the deeper question of "What is it all for?" He backs up his perspectives with primary research, valid scientific evidence, and detailed explanations of the long history of self-directed childhoods.

In his 2013 book, *Free to Learn*: Why Unleashing the Instinct to Play Will Make Our Children Happier, More Self-Reliant, and Better Students for Life, Dr. Gray grounds his views in rigorous evolutionary research on the universal ways in which indigenous hunters and gatherers raised their young. His analysis shows that children are healthiest and learn most effectively when they are left to playfully explore their natural curiosities in a nurturing environment equipped with the tools of their culture. Dr. Gray observes that for hundreds of thousands of years, constituting nearly all of human history, this was the way in which children were raised. In other words, our species has survived throughout nearly all of our history by being trustful parents, and allowing children to self direct their own childhoods. This realization has given me, and many others, the knowledge and courage to depart and divest from the unnatural, unhealthy, and unjust attitude toward childhood that prevails in most cultures today.

Peter Gray's dedication and contribution to the subject of children's rights has inspired a new generation of advocates, now equipped with his scientific evidence of what is the long-established, just, and healthy way for children to thrive in their development. This compendium of essays, assembled and adapted from his column "Freedom to Learn," appearing in *Psychology Today*, presents the many years of findings and reporting of Dr. Gray's lifelong work. It is a contemporary reader's great fortune to have this compilation available for inspiration and documentation. And it is my great honor to provide you with this work, which also initiates a hopefully long tradition of forthcoming books about the rights of the child. This compendium marks the inaugural publication of Tipping Points Press, dedicated to the advocacy of children's rights, by the Alliance for Self-Directed Education, which Peter Gray helped to found. We look forward to the continuation of pushing forward in advocating for children's rights until we reach that tipping point, when all children are free.

> *Alexander Khost*
> Editor-in-Chief
> Tipping Points Press
> The Alliance for Self-Directed Education
> APRIL 18, 2020

Author's Preface

I have been writing a blog for *Psychology Today* magazine, called "Freedom to Learn," since July, 2008. I have been posting there, at a rate of roughly one per month, articles dealing with child development and education, especially with children's natural ways of educating themselves when they are free to do so.

Over the years I have received many requests, from readers, for bound collections of these articles, arranged by topic, which would make the articles easier to find and easier to give to others than is possible by searching the *Psychology Today* online contents. Now, in collaboration with Tipping Points Press, the new book-publishing arm of the Alliance for Self-Directed Education (ASDE), I am responding to that request.

We are beginning with four collections, published simultaneously. The collection you have in hand is about the evidence that Self-Directed Education works (that children in charge of their own education educate themselves well). The other collections in this first set deal, respectively, with the harm to children that is perpetrated by our system of compulsory schooling; how children acquire academic skills (especially literacy and numeracy) when allowed to do so in their own ways; and the natural, biological drives that underlie children's self-education and the conditions that optimize those drives. The essays have in some cases been modified slightly from the original *Psychology Today* versions, for clarity and to add more recent information.

I thank Rachel Wallach for her excellent, volunteer work in copyediting this collection; Zaki Clements, who is a young person engaged in Self-Directed Education, for creating the cover illustration; and Alexander Khost, Editor-in-Chief of Tipping Point Press, for making these collections possible. I also thank the editors of *Psychology Today* for their support over the years in my posting these articles.

All profits from the sales of this book and others in the set help support ASDE in its mission to make opportunities for Self-Directed Education available to all families that seek it.

Peter Gray

1

Children Educate Themselves I

Outline of Some of the Evidence

*Children are designed by
nature for self-education*

JULY 16, 2008

As adults we do have certain responsibilities toward our children and the world's children. It is our responsibility to create
safe, health-promoting, respectful environments in which
children can develop. It is our responsibility to be sure that
children have proper foods, fresh air, non-toxic places to play,
and lots of opportunities to interact freely with people of all
ages. It is our responsibility to be models of human decency.
But one thing we do not have to worry about is how to educate
children.

We do not have to worry about curricula, lesson plans,
motivating children to learn, testing them, and all the rest
that comes under the rubric of pedagogy. Let's turn that
energy, instead, toward creating decent environments in

1

which children can play. Children's education is children's responsibility, not ours. Only they can do it. They are built to do it. Our task regarding education is just to stand back and let it happen. The more we try to control it, the more we interfere.

When I say that education is children's responsibility and that they are, by nature, designed to assume that responsibility, I do not expect you to take that assertion on faith. We live in a world in which that assertion is not the self-evident truth that it once was. We live in a world in which almost all children and adolescents are sent to school, beginning at ever-younger ages and ending at ever-older ages, and in which "school" has a certain standard meaning. We measure education in terms of scores on tests and success in advancing through the school system from one level to the next. Naturally, then, we come almost automatically to think of education as something that is done at schools by specialists trained in the art and science of pedagogy, who know how to put children through the paces that will turn their raw potential into an educated product.

So, I take it as my task to present evidence to support my claim. The most direct lines of evidence come from settings where we can see children educating themselves without anything resembling what we think of as schooling. Here are three such settings, which I will elaborate on in subsequent essays.

1. A huge amount of children's education occurs before they start school. The most obvious evidence of children's capacity for self-education, available to any of us who opens

our eyes, comes from watching kids in their first four or five years of life, before anyone tries in any systematic way to teach them anything. Think of all they learn in that period. They learn to walk, run, jump, climb. They learn about the physical properties of, and how to manipulate, all of the objects that are within their reach. They learn their native language, which is surely one of the most cognitively complex tasks that any human being ever masters. They learn the basic psychology of other people—how to please others, how to annoy them, how to get what they need or want from them. They learn all this not through lessons provided by anyone, but through their own free play, their insatiable curiosity, and their natural attentiveness to the behavior of other people. We can't stop them from learning all this and more unless we lock them up in closets.

2. Children in hunter-gatherer cultures become successful adults without anything like schooling. During most of human existence we lived in relatively small nomadic, foraging bands. Our basic human nature—including our playfulness, curiosity, and all of our other biological adaptations for learning—evolved in the context of that way of life. Some groups of hunter-gatherers managed to survive, with their cultures intact, into recent times. Anthropologist who have studied such groups—in Africa, Asia, South America, and elsewhere—have found a remarkable consistency across them in their attitudes toward children. In all of these cultures, children and adolescents are

permitted to play and follow their own interests, without adult interference, essentially from dawn to dusk every day. The belief of these people, borne out by millennia of experience, is that young people teach themselves through play and exploration and then, when ready to do so, begin naturally to put what they have learned to purposes that benefit the group as a whole. Through their own efforts, hunter-gatherer children acquire the enormous sets of skills and knowledge they need to be successful adults in their culture.

3. Children at certain "non-school schools" in our culture become successful adults without anything like conventional schooling. I have for many years been an observer of children and adolescents at the Sudbury Valley School, in Framingham, Massachusetts. The school was founded in 1968 by people whose beliefs about education are remarkably similar to those of hunter-gatherers. The school is for young people aged four through high school age, and it is nothing at all like a typical school. It is a democratic setting in which children have equal power to the adults and in which students learn entirely through their own self-directed activities. It is, essentially, a safe environment in which young people can play, explore, assume responsibility, and interact freely with others across the whole range of ages. There are no tests, no gold stars or other such rewards, no passing or failing, no required courses or coursework, no coercion or coaxing of children to learn, no expectations that the staff are responsible for

children's learning. By now, many hundreds of young people have educated themselves in this environment. And, no, they don't become hunters and gatherers. They become artisans, artists, chefs, doctors, engineers, entrepreneurs, lawyers, musicians, scientists, social workers, software designers, and so on. They can be found in the whole range of careers that we value in our culture.

In the next three essays I will elaborate, one by one, on these three sources of evidence about young people's capacities for self-education.

2

Children Educate Themselves II
We All Know That's True for Little Kids

Watching young children learn can revolutionize our views on education

JULY 22, 2008

Have you ever stopped to think about how much children learn in their first few years of life, before they start school, before anyone tries in any systematic way to teach them anything? Their learning comes naturally; it results from their instincts to play, explore, and observe others around them. But to say that it comes naturally is not to say that it comes effortlessly. Infants and young children put enormous energy into their learning. Their capacities for sustained attention, for physical and mental effort, and for overcoming frustrations and barriers are extraordinary. Next time you are in viewing range of a child under the age of about five years old, sit back and watch for awhile. Try to imagine what is going on in the child's mind each moment in his or her interactions with the world. If you allow yourself that luxury, you are in for a treat.

The experience might lead you to think about education in a whole new light—a light that shines from within the child rather than on the child.

Here I will sketch out a tiny bit of what developmental psychologists have learned about young children's learning. To help relate this knowledge to thoughts about education, I'll organize the sketch into categories of physical, linguistic, scientific, and social-moral education.

Physical Education

Let's begin with learning to walk. Walking on two legs is a species-typical trait of human beings. In some sense we are born for it. But even so, it doesn't come easily. Every human being who comes into the world puts enormous effort into learning to walk.

I remember one spring day long ago when my son, somewhere near his first birthday, was at the stage where he could walk by holding onto something but could not take steps alone. We happened to be traveling that day on a large tourist boat on the Hudson River in New York, and my son insisted on spending the entire ride walking up and down the deck while holding my hand. We spent many hours walking the length of the boat, with me uncomfortably stooped over so my hand could reach his. The motivation, of course, was entirely his. I was just a convenient tool, a human walking stick. I kept trying to convince him to take a rest because I needed one, but he was a master at manipulating me back into walking whenever we did stop for a moment.

Researchers have found that toddlers at the peak of learning to walk spend, on average, six hours per day walking, during which time they take an average of 9,000 steps and travel the length of 29 football fields (Adolph et al., 2003). They aren't trying to get anywhere in particular, they are just walking for the sake of walking. They become especially interested in walking when they are exposed to a new kind of surface. I suspect that my son on our boat ride was stimulated to walk partly because the boat's motion made walking more difficult and added a new and exciting challenge.

Early in the stage of walking alone, children often fall and sometimes hurt themselves, but then they pull themselves right back up and try again—and again, and again, and again. After walking comes running, jumping, climbing, swinging, and all sorts of new ways of moving. We don't have to teach children any of this, and we certainly don't have to motivate them. All we have to do is provide appropriate safe places for them to practice.

Language Education

If you have ever tried to learn a new language as an adult, you know how difficult it is. There are thousands of words to learn and countless grammatical rules. Yet children more or less master their native language by the age of four. By that age, in conversations, they exhibit a sophisticated knowledge of word meanings and grammatical rules. In fact, children growing up in bilingual homes acquire two languages by the age of four and somehow manage to keep them distinct.

Four-year-olds can't describe the grammatical rules of

their language (nor can most adults), but their implicit knowledge of the rules is clear in their speech and understanding. They add s to brand new nouns to make them plural, add ed to brand new verbs to put them into the past tense, and manifest an understanding of grammatical categories—nouns, verbs, adjectives, adverbs, and so on—in their construction of novel sentences. Infants may come into the world with some innate understanding of language, as Noam Chomsky long ago suggested, but the specific words and rules of every language are different and clearly have to be learned.

Infants and young children continuously educate themselves about language. Early in infancy they begin babbling language-like sounds, practicing the motor acts of articulation. With time they restrict their babbling more and more to the sounds of the specific language that they hear around them. By a few months of age, they can be observed to pay close attention to the speech of others and to engage in activities that seem to be designed to help them figure out what others are saying. For example, they regularly follow the eyes of older children or adults to see what the others are looking at, which helps them guess what they are talking about. With this strategy, a toddler in the garden who hears someone say, "What a pretty chrysanthemum," has a good chance of identifying what object is being referred to. Between the ages of two and seventeen, young people learn an average of about 60,000 words (Bloom, 2001); that works out to nearly one new word for every hour that they are awake.

Language learning, like learning to walk, is play. It is absorbing, intense, and done for its own sake. Young children go around naming things just for the fun of naming them, not for any other reward. And as children grow older their word play becomes ever more sophisticated, taking such forms as riddles, puns, and rhymes. We can't teach children language; all we can do is provide a normal human environment within which they can learn it and practice it, that is, an environment in which they can engage themselves with people who speak.

Science Education

Young children are enormously curious about all aspects of the world around them. Even within their first few days of life, infants spend more time looking at new objects than at those they have seen before. By the age at which they have enough eye-hand coordination to reach out and manipulate objects, they do just that—constantly. Six-month-olds examine every new object they can reach, in ways that are well-designed to learn about its physical properties. They squeeze it, pass it from hand to hand, look at it from all sides, shake it, and drop it to see what happens; and whenever something interesting happens they try to repeat it, as if to prove that it wasn't a fluke. Watch a six-month-old in action and see a scientist.

The primary goal of young people's exploration is to learn how to control their environment. Many experiments have shown that infants and young children are far more interested in objects whose actions they can control than in those they cannot control. For instance, an audio player that they can turn on and off through some effort of their own is far more fascinating to them than one that comes on and off by itself or is controlled by an adult. They are especially drawn to such objects during the period when they are learning how to control them. Once they have learned how to control an object and have exhausted all the possibilities for action on it, they tend to lose interest in it. That's why the cardboard carton that a fancy but uncontrollable toy comes in may sustain a child's interest for a longer time than the toy.

The drive to figure out how objects work and how to control them does not end with early childhood; it continues on as long as children and adults are free to follow their own paths. This drive is the foundation of science. Nothing destroys it more quickly than an environment in which everyone is told what they must do with new objects and how to do it. The fun of science lies in the discovery, not in the knowledge that results. That is true for all of us, whether we are 6-month-olds exploring a mobile, two-year-olds exploring a cardboard box, or adult scientists exploring the properties of a physical particle or an enzyme. Nobody goes into science because they like to be told the answers to someone else's questions; they go into science because they like to discover the answers to their own questions. That's why our standard method of training people in science never turns them into scientists. Those who become scientists do so despite such training.

Social and Moral Education

Even more fascinating to young children than the physical environment is the social environment. Children are naturally drawn to other children, especially to those others who are a little older than themselves and a little more competent. They want to do what those others do. They also want to play with others. Social play is the primary natural means of every child's social and moral education.

It is through play that children learn to get along with others. In play they must take into account the other children's needs, learn to see from others' points of view, learn to compromise, learn to negotiate differences, learn to control their own impulses, and learn to please others so as to keep them as playmates. These are all hard lessons, and they are among the most important lessons that all of us must learn if we are to live happy lives. We can't possibly teach these lessons to children; all we can do is let them play with others so they can experience, themselves, the consequences of their social failures and successes. The strong innate drive to play with others is what motivates children to work hard at getting along with others. Failure to get along ends the play, and that natural consequence is a powerful learning experience. No lectures or words of advice that we can provide can substitute for such experience.

What Happens to Motivation at Age 5 or 6?

Once, when my son was about seven years old and in public school, I mentioned to his teacher that he seemed to have been far more interested in learning before he started school than he was now. Her response was something like this: "Well, I'm sure you know, as a psychologist, that this is a natural developmental change. Children by nature are spontaneous learners when they are little, but then they become more task oriented."

I can understand where she got that idea. I've seen developmental psychology textbooks that divide the units according to age and refer to the preschool years as "the play years." All the discussion of play occurs in those first chapters. It is as if play stops at age five or six. The remaining chapters largely have to do with studies of how children perform on tasks that adults give them to perform. I imagine that the teacher had read such a book when she was taking education courses. But such books present a distorted view of what is natural. In the next two essays I will present evidence that when young people beyond the age of five or six are permitted the freedom and opportunities to follow their own interests, their drives to play and explore continue to motivate them, as strongly as ever, toward ever more sophisticated forms of learning.

References

Adolph, K. E., Vereijken, B., & Shrout, P. E. (2003). What changes in infant walking and why? *Child Development*, 74, 475-497.

Bloom, P., (2001). Précis of How children learn the meanings of words. *Behavioral & Brain Sciences*, 24, 1095-1103.

3

Children Educate Themselves III
The Wisdom of Hunter-Gatherers

How hunter-gatherer children
learn without schools

AUGUST 2, 2008

For hundreds of thousands of years, up until the time when agriculture was invented (a mere 10,000 years ago), we were all hunter-gatherers. Our human instincts, including all of the instinctive means by which we learn, came about in the context of that way of life. And so it is natural that in this series on children's instinctive ways of educating themselves I should ask: How do hunter-gatherer children learn what they need to know to become effective adults within their culture?

In the last half of the 20th century, anthropologists located and observed many groups of people—in remote parts Africa, Asia, Australia, New Guinea, South America, and elsewhere—who had maintained a hunting-and-gathering life, almost unaffected by modern ways. Although each group studied had its own language and other cultural traditions, the various groups were found to be similar in many basic ways, which allows us to speak of "the hunter-gatherer way of life" in the singular. Wherever they were found, hunter-gatherers lived in small nomadic bands (of about 25 to 50 people per band), made decisions democratically, had ethical systems that centered on egalitarian values and sharing, and had rich cultural traditions that included music, art, games, dances, and time-honored stories.

To supplement what we could find in the anthropological literature, several years ago Jonathan Ogas (then a graduate student) and I contacted a number of anthropologists who had lived among hunter-gatherers and asked them to respond to a written questionnaire about their observations of children's lives. Ten such scholars kindly responded to our questionnaire. Among them, they had studied seven different hunter-gatherer cultures—four in Africa, one in Malaysia, one in the Philippines, and one in New Guinea.

Four Conclusions About Children's Education in Hunter-Gatherer Cultures

What I learned from my reading and our questionnaire was startling for its consistency across different hunter-gatherer groups. Here I will summarize four conclusions, which I think are most relevant to the issue of self-education (for more, see Gray 2012). Because I would like you to picture these practices as occurring now, I will use the present tense in describing them, even though the practices and the cul-

tures themselves have been largely destroyed in recent years
by intrusions from the more "developed" world around them.

1. Hunter-gatherer children must learn an enormous
   amount to become successful adults. It would be a mistake to think that education is not a big deal for hunter-
   gatherers because they don't have to learn much. In fact,
   they have to learn an enormous amount.

   To become effective hunters, boys must learn the habits
   of the two or three hundred different species of mammals
   and birds that the band hunts, must know how to track
   such game using the slightest clues, must be able to craft
   perfectly the tools of hunting (such as bows and arrows,
   blowguns and darts, snares or nets), and must be extraor-
   dinarily skilled at using those tools.

   To become effective gatherers, girls must learn which
   of the countless varieties of roots, tubers, nuts, seeds,
   fruits, and greens in their area are edible and nutritious,
   when and where to find them, how to dig them (in the case
   of roots and tubers), how to extract the edible portions
   efficiently (in the case of grains, nuts, and certain plant
   fibers), and in some cases how to process them to make
   them edible or increase their nutritional value. These abilities include physical skills, honed by years of practice, as
   well as the capacity to remember, use, add to, and modify
   an enormous store of culturally shared verbal knowledge
   about the food materials.

   In addition, hunter-gatherer children must learn how
   to navigate their huge foraging territory, build huts, make

fires, cook, fend off predators, predict weather changes, treat wounds and diseases, assist births, care for infants, maintain harmony within their group, negotiate with neighboring groups, tell stories, make music, and engage in the various dances and rituals of their culture. Since there is generally little specialization beyond that of men as hunters and women as gatherers, each person must acquire a large fraction of the total knowledge and skills of the culture.

2. Hunter-gatherer children learn all this without being taught. Although hunter-gatherer children must learn an enormous amount, hunter-gatherers have nothing like school. Adults do not establish a curriculum, or attempt to motivate children to learn, or give lessons, or monitor children's progress. When asked how children learn what they need to know, hunter-gatherer adults invariably answer with words that mean essentially: "They teach themselves through their observations, play, and exploration." Occasionally an adult might offer a word of advice or demonstrate how to do something better, such as how to shape an arrowhead, but such help is given only when the child clearly desires it. Adults do not initiate, direct, or interfere with children's activities. Adults do not show any evidence of worry about their children's education; millennia of experience have proven to them that children are experts at educating themselves (see Gosso et al., 2005).

3. Hunter-gatherer children are afforded enormous amounts of time to play and explore. In response to our question

about how much time children had for play, the anthropologists we surveyed were unanimous in indicating that the hunter-gatherer children they observed were free to play most if not all of the day, every day. Typical responses are the following:

> "[Batek] children were free to play nearly all the time; no one expected children to do serious work until they were in their late teens." (Karen Endicott)

> "Both girls and boys [among the Nharo] had almost all day every day free to play." (Alan Barnard)

> "[Efé] boys were free to play nearly all the time until age 15-17; for girls most of the day, in between a few errands and some babysitting, was spent in play." (Robert Bailey)

> "[!Kung] children played from dawn to dusk." (Nancy Howell)

The freedom that hunter-gatherer children enjoy to pursue their own interests comes partly from the adults' understanding that such pursuits are the surest path to education. It also comes from the general spirit of egalitarianism and personal autonomy that pervades hunter-gatherer cultures and applies as much to children as to adults (Kent, 1996). Hunter-gatherer adults view children as complete individuals, with rights comparable to those of adults. Their assumption is that children will, of their own accord, begin contributing to the economy of the band when they are developmentally ready to do so. There is no need to make children or anyone else do what they don't want to do. It is remarkable to think that our instincts to learn and to contribute to the community evolved in a world in which our instincts were trusted!

4. Hunter-gatherer children observe adults' activities and incorporate those activities into their play. Hunter-gatherer children are never isolated from adult activities. They observe directly all that occurs in camp—the preparations to move, the building of huts, the making and mending of tools and other artifacts, the food preparation and cooking, the nursing and care of infants, the precautions taken against predators and diseases, the gossip and discussions, the arguments and politics, the dances and festivities. They sometimes accompany adults on food gathering trips, and by age 10 or so, boys sometimes accompany men on hunting trips.

   The children not only observe all of these activities, but they also incorporate them into their play, and through that play they become skilled at the activities. As they grow older, their play turns gradually into the real thing. There is no sharp division between playful participation and real participation in the valued activities of the group.

   For example, boys who one day are playfully hunting butterflies with their little bows and arrows are, on a later day, playfully hunting small mammals and bringing some of them home to eat, and on yet a later day are joining men on real hunting trips, still in the spirit of play. As another example, both boys and girls commonly build play huts, modeled after the real huts that the adults build. In her response to our questionnaire, Nancy Howell pointed out that !Kung children commonly build a whole village of play huts a few hundred yards from the real village. The play village then becomes a playground where they act out many of the kinds of scenes that they observe among adults.

The respondents to our survey referred also to many other examples of valued adult activities that were emulated regularly by children in play. Digging up roots, fishing, smoking porcupines out of holes, cooking, caring for infants, climbing trees, building vine ladders, using knives and other tools, making tools, carrying heavy loads, building rafts, making fires, defending against attacks from predators, imitating animals (a means of identifying animals and learning their habits), making music, dancing, story-telling, and arguing were all mentioned by one or more respondents. Because all this play occurs in an age-mixed environment, the smaller children are constantly learning from the older ones.

Nobody has to tell or encourage the children to do all this. They do it naturally because, like children everywhere, there is nothing that they desire more than to grow up and to be like the successful adults they see around them. The desire to grow up is a powerful motive that blends with the drives to play and explore and ensures that children, if given a chance, will practice endlessly the skills that they need to develop to become effective adults.

What Relevance Might These Observations Have for Education in Our Culture?

Our culture, of course, is very different from hunter-gatherer cultures. You might well doubt that the lessons about education that we learn from hunter-gatherers can be applied effectively in our culture today. For starters, hunter-gatherers do not have reading, writing, or arithmetic; maybe the natural, self-motivated means of learning don't work for learning the three Rs. In our culture, unlike in hunter-gatherer cultures, there are countless different ways of making a living, countless different sets of skills and knowledge that children might acquire, and it is impossible for children in their daily lives to observe all those adult skills directly. In our culture, unlike in hunter-gatherer cultures, children are largely segregated from the adult work world, which reduces their opportunities to see what adults do and incorporate those activities into their play.

Yet, in the next essay, I am going to argue that the same natural means of learning that work so well for hunter-gatherers indeed do work equally well for our children, when we provide an educational setting that allows those means to work. That essay is about a school in Framingham, Massachusetts, where, for decades, children and teens have been educating themselves with extraordinary success through their self-directed play and exploration.

References

Gosso, Y., et al. (2005), Play in hunter-gatherer societies. In A. D. Pellegrini & P. K. Smith (Eds.), *The nature of play: great apes and humans*. New York: Guilford.

Gray, P. (2012). The value of a play-filled childhood in development of the hunter-gatherer individual. In Narvaez, D., Panksepp, J., Schore, A., & Gleason, T. (Eds.), *Evolution, early experience and human development: from research to practice and policy.* New York: Oxford University Press,

Kent, S. (1996), Cultural diversity among African foragers: causes and implications. In S. Kent (Ed.), *Cultural diversity among twentieth-century foragers: an African perspective*. Cambridge, England: Cambridge University Press.

4

Children Educate Themselves IV

Lessons from Sudbury Valley

*Children have been educating themselves
successfully at this school for decades*

AUGUST 13, 2008

The Sudbury Valley School has, since its founding in 1968, been the best-kept secret in American education. Most students of education have never heard of it. Professors of education ignore it, not out of malice but because they cannot absorb it into their framework of educational thought. The Sudbury Valley model of education is not a variation of standard education. It is not a progressive version of traditional schooling. It is not a Montessori school or a Dewey school or a Piagetian constructivist school. It is something entirely different. To understand the school, one has to begin with a completely different mindset from that which dominates current educational thinking. One has to begin with the thought: Adults do not control children's education; children educate themselves.

But the secret is getting out, spread largely by students and others who have experienced the Sudbury Valley School directly. As of this writing, at least two dozen schools throughout the world are modeled after Sudbury Valley. I predict that at some future time—I hope within my lifetime, but perhaps that is optimistic—the Sudbury Valley model will be featured in every standard textbook of education and will be widely accepted as one of a number of normal educational routes. At some point today's approach to education will be seen by most as a barbaric remnant of the past. People will wonder why the world took so long to come to grips with such a simple and self-evident idea as that upon which the Sudbury Valley School is founded: Children educate themselves; we don't have to do it for them.

In the last post I summarized evidence that hunter-gatherer children learn the extraordinary amount that they must to become effective adults through their own self-directed play and exploration. In the post before that, I pointed out that children in our culture learn many of the most difficult lessons they will ever learn before they start school, entirely on their own initiatives, without adult direction or prodding. And now, based on the experiences of the Sudbury Valley School, I contend that self-education works just as well for school-aged children and adolescents in our culture as it does for preschoolers and for hunter-gatherers.

For many years I have had the opportunity to observe the Sudbury Valley School, both as the father of a student who went there and as an academician using the school as a resource to study play and self-directed learning. Here I'll tell you a little about the school.

First, a few mundane facts. The school was founded in 1968 and has been in continuous operation since then. It is a private day school, in Framingham, Massachusetts, open to students age four through high-school age. The school is not in any sense elitist. It admits students without regard to any measures of academic performance, and it operates at a per pupil cost about half that of the surrounding public schools. The school typically has about 150 students and 7 or 8 adult staff members. It is housed in a large Victorian house and a remodeled barn, which sit on ten acres of land in a part of town that was largely rural when the school began operating and retains a rural flavor. Now, the more remarkable facts concerning the school's mode of operation:

The School Operates as a Participatory Democracy

The Sudbury Valley School is first and foremost a community in which children and adolescents experience directly the privileges and responsibilities of democratic government. The primary administrative body is the School Meeting, which consists of all students and staff members. In one-person-one-vote fashion, the School Meeting, which meets once a week, creates all of the school's rules, establishes committees to oversee the school's day-to-day operation, and hires and fires staff members. Four-year-olds at the school have the same vote as older students and adult staff members in all of this.

No staff members at the school have tenure. All are on one-year contracts, which must be renewed each year through a secret-ballot election. As the student voters outnumber the staff by a factor of about 20 to 1, the staff members who survive this process and are re-elected year after year are those who are admired by the students. They are people who are kind, ethical, and competent, and who contribute significantly and positively to the school's environment. They are adults that the students may wish in some ways to emulate.

The school's rules are enforced by the Judicial Committee, which changes regularly in membership but always includes a staff member and students representing the full range of ages at the school. When a student or staff member is charged by another school member with violating a rule, the accuser and the accused must appear before the Judicial Committee, which determines innocence or guilt and, in the latter case, decides on an appropriate sentence. In all of this, staff members are treated in the same way as students. Nobody is above the law.

The School Does not Interfere with Students' Activities

Students are free, all day, every day, to do what they wish at the school, as long as they don't violate any of the school's rules. The rules, all made by the School Meeting, have to do with protecting the school and protecting students' opportunities to pursue their own interests unhindered by others. School members must not make noise in designated "quiet

rooms," misuse equipment or fail to put it away when finished, deface school property, use illegal drugs on campus,
or behave in any way toward another person that makes that
person feel harassed. Behaviors of those sorts are the fodder
of Judicial Committee complaints.

None of the school's rules have to do with learning. The
school gives no tests. It does not evaluate or grade students'
progress. There is no curriculum and no attempt to motivate
students to learn. Courses occur only when students take the
initiative to organize them, and they last only as long as the
students want them. Many students at the school never join
a course, and the school sees no problem with that. The staff
members at the school do not consider themselves to be teachers. They are, instead, adult members of the community who
provide a wide variety of services, including some teaching.
Most of their "teaching" is of the same variety as can be found
in any human setting; it involves answering sincere questions
and presenting ideas in the context of real conversations.

The school is a rich environment for play and exploration, and therefore for learning

Learning at Sudbury Valley is largely incidental. It occurs as
a side effect of students' self-directed play and exploration.
The school is a wonderful place to play, explore, and, more
generally, to find and pursue one's interests. It provides space
and time. It also provides equipment—including computers,
a fully equipped kitchen, a woodworking shop, an art room,
playground equipment, toys and games of various sorts, and

many books. Students also have access to a pond, a field, and a nearby forest for outdoor play and exploration. Those who develop a special interest that needs some new piece of equipment might convince the School Meeting to buy it, or they might raise the money and buy it themselves by some means such as baking and selling cookies in the school.

The most important resource at the school, for most students, is other students, who among them manifest an enormous range of interests and abilities. Because of the free age mixing, students are exposed regularly to the activities and ideas of others who are older and younger than themselves. Age-mixed play offers younger children continuous opportunities to learn from older ones. For example, many students at the school have learned to read as a side effect of playing games (including computer games) that involve written words with students who already know how to read. They may learn to read without even being aware that they are doing so.

Much of the students' exploration at the school, especially that of the teenagers, takes place through conversations. Students talk about everything imaginable, with each other and with staff members, and through such talk they are exposed to a huge range of ideas and arguments. Because nobody is an official authority, everything that is said and heard in conversation is understood as something to think about, not as dogma to memorize or feed back on a test. Conversation, unlike memorizing for a test, stimulates the intellect. The great Russian psychologist Lev Vygotsky argued, long ago, that conversation is the foundation for higher thought, and observations of students at Sudbury Valley convince me that he was right. Thought is internalized conversation; external conversation, with other people, gets it started.

Hundreds of Graduates Attest to the School's Educational Effectiveness

My own first study of the Sudbury Valley School, many years ago, was a follow-up of the graduates (Gray & Chanoff, 1986; see also Gray, 2017). Since that time, the school itself has conducted several surveys of graduates, which have been published as books (available through the Sudbury Valley School Press). All of these studies have shown that the school works well as an educational institution.

Graduates of Sudbury Valley can be found today in the whole range of careers that are valued by our society. Their numbers include skilled craftspeople, entrepreneurs, artists, musicians, scientists, social workers, nurses, doctors, and so on. Those who chose to pursue higher education had no particular difficulties getting into colleges and universities, including highly selective ones, or performing well there once admitted. Many others have become successful in careers without going to college. More important, former students report that they are happy with their lives. They are almost unanimous in reporting that they are glad that they attended Sudbury Valley and in believing that the school prepared them better than a traditional school would have for the realities of adult existence. To a considerable degree they maintain, in adulthood, the playful (and that means focused and intense as well as joyful) attitude about careers and life that they developed and refined while at the school.

References

Gray, P. (2017). Self-directed education—unschooling and democratic schooling. In G. Noblit (Ed.), *Oxford research encyclopedia of education*. New York: Oxford University Press.

Gray, P., & Chanoff, D. (1986). Democratic schooling: What happens to young people who have charge of their own education? *American Journal of Education*, 94, 182-213.

5

The Benefits of Unschooling

Report I from a Large Survey

*What, to unschoolers, are the
benefits of skipping school?*

FEBRUARY 28, 2012

In September, 2011, I posted an essay on my *Psychology Today* blog introducing readers to the unschooling movement and inviting unschooling families to participate in a survey. The invitation was also posted on Patrick Farenga's Learning Without Schooling website and Jan Hunt's Natural Child Project website. The questionnaire emailed to those who responded asked them to tell us a bit about their family, including the age and sex of each child, the employment of each parent, and the history of schooling, homeschooling, and unschooling of each child. It also asked the respondents to define unschooling as it was practiced in their home, to describe the path that led them to unschooling, and to tell us about the biggest challenges and benefits of that educational route for their family. My colleague Gina Riley (professor of education at Hunter College) and I subsequently analyzed the results for academic publication (for the resulting publication, see Gray & Riley, 2013).

Here, in a series of three posts, my intention is to present a more informal report of the survey results, which will include many direct quotations from the survey responses, which couldn't be done in the more formal academic article. In this first post, I present some general statistics about the families who responded and then focus on their definitions of unschooling and their statements about the benefits of unschooling. In subsequent posts I'll focus on their paths to unschooling and the biggest challenges of that route to education.

Who responded to the survey?

In all, 255 families responded to the survey. However, for 23 of these families the oldest child had not yet reached school age (which we took to be 5 years old), and we chose not to include those families for the purpose of our main analyses. This left us with 232 unschooling families. Of these, 187 were from the United States, 19 were from Canada, and the remaining 26 were from other countries, mostly in Europe. The respondents from the US came from 34 different states, the most frequently represented of which are California (23), New York (14), and Oregon (10).

Of the 232 families, 48 had one child, 104 had two children, 51 had three, and the rest had four or more. In the great majority of families (221 of them), the person who filled out the questionnaire was the mother, in nine families it was the father, and in two it was an unschooled child who was an adult at the time of the survey. Most (210) of the families appeared to be two-parent families (as best as we could judge from the questionnaires), with both parents (or one parent and a step-parent) living at home. Twenty-one families were headed by single mothers, and one was headed by a single father.

Concerning employment, roughly half of the mothers identified themselves as stay-at-home moms (often with part-time jobs), and the remaining were relatively evenly split among those employed as professionals of one type or another, self-employed entrepreneurs, and "other." The great majority of the fathers were employed full time and were also relatively evenly split among professionals, self-employed entrepreneurs, and other.

It should be clear to anyone reading this report that this is not a random sample of all unschoolers. Rather, the respondents are those who in one way or another found the survey form and took the trouble to fill it out and email it to me. One might expect that, as a whole, these are among the most enthusiastic unschoolers—the ones who are most eager to share their experiences. The general claims I make here apply only to the group who responded, not necessarily to the whole population of unschoolers.

How did the respondents define unschooling?

In the announcement of the survey, I defined unschooling as not schooling and then elaborated by saying: "Unschoolers do not send their children to school and they do not do at home the kinds of things that are done at school. More specifically, they do not establish a curriculum for their children, do not require their children to do particular assignments for the purpose of education, and do not test their children to measure progress. Instead, they allow their children freedom to pursue their own interests and to learn, in their own ways, what they need to know to follow those interests. They also, in various ways, provide an environmental context and environmental support for the child's learning. Life and learning do not occur in a vacuum; they occur in the context of a cultural environment, and unschooling parents help define and bring the child into contact with that environment."

To find out how the families themselves defined unschooling I asked: "Please describe briefly how your family defines unschooling. What if any responsibility do you, as parent(s), assume for the education of your children?"

Essentially all of the respondents emphasized the role of their children in directing their own education and in pointing out that education is not separate from life itself. The responses varied, however, in the ways they described the parents' roles. We coded the responses, somewhat arbitrarily, into three categories—which I'll simply refer to as Categories 1, 2, and 3—according to the degree to which they mentioned deliberate roles the parents played in guiding and/or motivating their child's education. I should emphasize that these categories do not have to do with the degree to which the parents are involved in the child's daily lives, but just with the degree to which that involvement, according to the parents' descriptions, was deliberately directed toward the child's education.

By our coding, 101 (44 percent) of the responses fell into Category 1. These were the responses that most strongly emphasized the role of the child and did not describe parental activities conducted specifically for the purpose of the child's education, other than being responsive to the child's wishes or the child's lead. As illustration, one respondent in this category wrote: "Unschooling equals freedom in learning and in life. We push aside paradigms and established regulations with regards to schooling and trust our children to pave their own way in their own educations. Everything they want to experience has value. We trust them." Another wrote: "Unschooling, for us, means there is absolutely no curriculum, agenda, timetable, or goal setting. The children are responsible for what, how, and when they learn."

By our coding, 96 (41 percent) of the responses fell into Category 2. These differed from Category 1 only in that they made some mention of deliberate parental roles in guiding or motivating their children's education. As illustration, one in this category wrote: "We define unschooling as creating an enriching environment for our children where natural learning and passions can flourish. We want our life to be about connection—to each other, to our interests and passions, to a joyful life together. . . As a parent, I am my children's experienced partner and guide and I help them to gain access to materials and people that they might not otherwise have access to. I introduce them to things, places, people that I think might be interesting to them, but I do not push them or feel rejected or discouraged if they do not find it interesting."

Finally, 35 (15 percent) of the responses fell into Category 3. These were responses that might be considered as falling at the borderline between unschooling and what is sometimes called "relaxed homeschooling." The parents in these cases seemed to have at least some relatively specific educational goals in mind for their children and seemed to work deliberately toward achieving those goals. As illustration, one in this category wrote: "We believe that, for the most part, our daughter should be encouraged to explore subjects that are of interest to her, and it is our responsibility as parents to make learning opportunities available to her. . . I usually ask her to learn something or do something new or educational every day (and I explain to her why learning something new every day is such a cool thing to do!)."

What, to these families, are the benefits of unschooling?

The question about benefits came last in the questionnaire. It was worded as follows: "What, for your family, have been the biggest benefits of unschooling?" This was the question that led to the most prolific and often eloquent answers. The most common categories of benefits were the following:

1. Learning advantages for the child. One hundred and thirty-three (57 percent) of the respondents mentioned benefits that fell into this category. They said that their children were learning more, or learning more efficiently, or learning more relevant material, or learning more eagerly in the unschooling situation than they would if they were in school or being schooled at home. Many in this category said that because their children were in charge of their own learning, their curiosity and eagerness to learn remained intact.

2. Emotional and social advantages for the child. One hundred and twenty-one (52 percent) of the respondents mentioned benefits that fell in this category. They said that their children were happier, less stressed, more self-confident, more agreeable, or more socially outgoing than they would be if they were in school or being schooled at home. Many in this category referred to the social advantages of age mixing; their children interacted regularly with people of all ages in the community, not just with kids their own age as they would if they were in school.

3. Family closeness. One hundred and thirty-two (57 percent) mentioned benefits that fell in this category. They wrote that because of unschooling they could spend more time together as a family, do what they wanted to together, and that the lack of hassle over homework or other schooling issues promoted warm, harmonious family relationships.

4. Family freedom from the schooling schedule. Eighty-four (36 percent) mentioned benefits in this category. They said that freedom from the school's schedule allowed the children and the family as a whole to operate according to more natural rhythms of their own choice and take trips that would otherwise be impossible. Some also mentioned that because of the free schedule, their kids could get jobs or participate in community projects that would be impossible if they had to be in school during the day.

A Sample of Quotations About the Benefits of Unschooling

The remainder of this essay consists of 33 quotations, from the questionnaires, about the benefits of unschooling. The quotations reflect the views and the enthusiasm of these unschooling families much better than any paraphrasing I could provide. Each quotation comes from a different questionnaire.

"Wow. . . this list could be miles long! More time together, less arguing, watching our daughter spend hours absorbed in things that she is pursuing on her own, seeing her getting enough sleep and not coming down with viruses that she used to catch at school, exploring museums and other community resources together, talking as a family every day, not rushing in the morning, no homework, no mandatory school functions, no dysfunctional school social environment, no lunch to pack, no papers to fill out and send back every day, no fundraising, seeing our daughter happy with who she is and what she is doing, not worrying about tests/grades/teachers' opinions, and spending money that used to be spent on tuition or curriculum supplies on things that she truly wants to learn about. The biggest, number one benefit has to be our family relationships, though. What a difference now that we actually have time for each other! School did not just keep [our child] busy; it overwhelmed the whole family."

"Children who are full of joy, full of love for learning, creative, self-directed, passionate, enthusiastic, playful, thoughtful, questioning, and curious. Siblings who are very good friends. Close family bond among all of us. Lots of time together. Ability to experience and explore the world."

"Oh my, the benefits are enormous. Lifelong curiosity, family closeness, extraordinary success as my children step into academia and careers, and the empowerment that comes with being oneself in a world relentlessly telling us that we're only what we look like or own. I see it every weekend when my college kids are home and my research biologist daughter is back from work. They sit at the table long after dinner is over, talking about their admittedly esoteric interests and bantering as only those who love each other do. Then, even as adults, they push away from the table to go work on a project together, something that has bonded them for years. As the day stretches out, they finally gather on the porch, reluctant to part, still conversing and planning and laughing. I can't imagine greater riches."

"Enjoying a family-centered life rather than an institution-centered life has been the biggest benefit of unschooling. Our late riser can rise late and our early morning lover can get up early. We don't need to wrap our lives around the schedule of a school. Our kids learn all the time, instead of being trained to learn one subject at a time in 50-minute increments book-ended by bells. We are incredibly fortunate to live in a time and place where we enjoy the free life of unschooling."

"The other big benefit is that my kids have such a love of learning and of life, which was never destroyed by conventional school. So we don't have the kind of power struggles that other parents seem to have over bedtimes and homework. . . After all, happy relationships should ideally not be based on power issues. I can truly say that we are free of that, and that we spend time together as a family not because we are forced to, but because we enjoy it and love each other. What could be better than that?"

"Seeing the kids learn things naturally, and at their own pace without forcing them. Seeing the amount of creativity and imagination my kids have because they aren't expected to conform and be followers. Seeing them become very involved and interested in subjects that I wouldn't have imagined."

"When I am around friends whose kids are in school, I am struck by how much of their lives center around school. Get to bed so you can get up so you can be there on time, pack lunch, get home so you can do homework, organize all your stuff so you'll have it the next day. There are so many disagreements and struggles around all of this stuff—YUCK. It's life-changing just not having to have a schedule and nag everyone all the time to keep up with it!"

"The children can delve deeper into subjects that matter to them, spend longer on topics that interest them . . . The children can participate in the real world, learn real life skills, converse with people of all ages. They do not have to waste time with endless review, boring homework, having to work above or beneath their abilities, or in unpleasant power dynamics with adults with whom they have no connection. They can be themselves, and learn about themselves, and become who they truly want to be."

"The world, and all of its amazing opportunities, truly is my children's playground. My husband and I firmly believe that if our children have freedom and the opportunity to explore and follow their interests now that, as they mature and have to work, they will have a much better chance of truly knowing what they would like to do and will find their careers and adult life both worthwhile and enjoyable."

"Watching our daughter relax and enjoy her days is immensely satisfying, especially against the backdrop of her past few schooled years. The freedom from school and its expectations, the freedom to be, to live, has been liberating for all of us."

"Watching my children learn so much so effortlessly. I watched my 5-year-old daughter teach herself to read and write. It was the most amazing thing to watch. It was like she was a code breaker."

"The biggest benefits have been witnessing our daughters' creativity blossom full force, their ability to think outside the box when presented with problems, their resourcefulness, and their genuine desire to ask questions and learn as much as they can about the world around them. Also, seeing them internalize the lesson that making mistakes is a necessary and wonderful platform for growth and further learning, which means they see mistakes as a positive and necessary part of their education. They're not afraid to try their hand at just about anything."

"Trust! This unschooling path has taught me to trust my instincts and to trust my children to know what feels right to them. There is no perfect life but mistakes are our mirror to see what we would have done differently and how we will decide now with the knowledge we have."

"The list is endless. Most important: that learning was simply a normal part of everyday life, as natural and as necessary as breathing—never something confined to a specific place or time. But also: being able to spend so much time together, getting to know each other so well. Being able to travel whenever we wanted (useful when the girls began fencing competitively, too—we never had to worry about school releases). That the girls OWNED their learning, despite their occasional doubts. By the time they reached adulthood, they knew how to go about learning anything they were interested in because they'd been able to do that all their lives. That the girls grew up curious and could indulge that curiosity. That the girls were not subjected to school textbooks and could read what we still think of as 'real' books. That the girls learned for themselves how to organize and prioritize their time and energy to get things done. That we had the leisure not only to learn what and where we wanted, but to figure out the best ways we learned, which could change from year to year and subject to subject. That nobody had to ask permission for bathroom breaks. That we could eat while we read if we wanted to."

"The curiosity that he had as a 3 or 4-year-old is still there. He thinks life is interesting and fun. He has confidence in his ability to do anything he wants to do."

"A huge reduction in stress for our kids and me . . . being able to sleep and eat on our own natural schedule . . . learning at their own pace, in ways that work best for them, information and skills that they chose to learn, and therefore coming to enjoy learning!"

"Freedom! [My children] got to live as free people, and blossomed as individuals! They had the time to figure out who they are, what they enjoy and are interested in; had opportunities to learn and do all kinds of interesting things that schooled children typically don't have time for; were free from the bullying and threats (from the teachers) at school; and had a group of homeschooled friends who were/are very nice, generally happy and optimistic, friendly, interesting and interested people."

"Another huge benefit is that [my son's] stress levels are way down, and he is happy. I realized by keeping him in school, I was stifling his creativity, his passions, and teaching him he must put those things on the back burner and conform to what society thinks is best for him to learn. . . He wants to work and make money, and now he is also free to contribute to society in a valuable way instead of being in a classroom all day."

"I got my son back. The school wanted him 'diagnosed' with something he doesn't have. . . he's just a super creative, intensely sensitive kid who has so much to offer the world just as he is. He has never had a problem getting along with other kids. He makes friends everywhere he goes and is still in touch with his school friends, too. Unschooling has been such a blessing for us. It has taken the stress off of my son (as well as me) and allows him to follow his bliss and to create and imagine and think for himself. He reads better now than he ever did in school."

"One example is that of control. My youngest is a walking power struggle; she can turn any moment into a fight for control. By allowing her education to be her choice and responsibility, we have a far better relationship and she spends her energy learning instead of fighting. (We have enough to fight over with whether she will brush her teeth or wear weather-appropriate clothes, after all.)"

"I feel like I'm trying to answer a question about the benefits of breathing. We don't have to schedule, assume, judge, direct, or anxiously evaluate. We just get to enjoy each other. My son gets to live a life focused on what he loves at the moment."

"I love watching my kids grow and learn and ask questions. I love having one less thing to worry about (finding the time for "school") and I love being able to skip curriculum shopping and planning. I also look around at other homeschoolers and feel sorry for their constant stress and worry (Is my kid learning enough? Did we pick the right curriculum? How much does homeschooling cost?). I see traditional homeschoolers so burned out by the stress they make for themselves. Don't they know their kids will learn despite them?"

"Hands down, the relationship with our kids has flourished. We have never gone through the typical teen angst or rebellion so often touted as normal. I don't think it is. If you build up your family life where members work together and help one another, where the focus is on happy learning, it's hard NOT to get along and enjoy each other's company! Schools have an insidious way of pitting parents against kids and eroding the relationship that could flourish outside of that environment. When kids, and all people really, can relax and enjoy life and learn and pursue interests, they are happy. When people are happy, they get along better, they work together and inspire one another, learn from one another, and grow stronger and healthier. All of that has spilled over into marital life and all family relationships, including siblings. I knew without a doubt that the learning would happen and that it would be amazing! I didn't expect the stark difference in our relationship with our kids, as compared to what I thought it should be like by what I saw in other families with kids in school."

"Watching our children's interest in learning grow rather than diminish, and seeing them use their knowledge regularly in conversation and in play with others, rather than dumping it after a test."

"The happiness and joy we experience every day is the biggest benefit. Our lives are essentially stress free since we are living the way we want by making the choices that feel good for us. We have a very close relationship built on love, mutual trust, and mutual respect. As an educator I see that my daughter has amazing critical thinking skills that many of my adult college students lack... My daughter lives and learns in the real world and loves it. What more could I ask for?"

"Looking at my grown children, I can see that both are securely self-motivated, both are much more social and outgoing than I was at their ages, and both are living lives they have crafted out of their own interests and talents. That is deeply satisfying. In addition, we all have a strong connection that has grown directly from our shared experiences throughout their childhoods."

"I have seen my sons' passions bloom. They are happy and expressive and take pride in themselves and their projects. They are knowledgeable about so many more things than are their schooled peers. They have a mindset that is not hampered by negativity or limitations, something more common with their schooled peers. They have big imaginations."

"My daughters are very creative and artistic, loved college way more (they reported) than their burned-out-about-institutions peers, are skeptical and generally science-minded, and are ethical people."

"Unschooling saved both my children's self-esteem, for different reasons. [My son] was pegged as a 'bad' kid at school, and had he continued down the path he was going (with the school and teachers openly hostile towards him), the damage school was causing him would have led him to self-medicate through alcohol and drugs by the time he was in high school. When we withdrew him from school, not only did his self-esteem return but the close, trusting relationship we had before he went to preschool returned. [My daughter] was diagnosed with learning disabilities and I was told she would never read on grade level and she was always going to need special services. Keeping her out of school and letting her learn at her own pace prevented her from a lifetime of feeling like she was stupid."

"Unschooling is not a panacea that prevents all unhappiness or difficulty; it's important not to oversimplify or romanticize this. Our daughters have had problems and struggles like all teenagers do in our society. They are extremely smart and well-educated, but I think that would be true if they had gone to school. I think the biggest difference is that they know themselves better than we did at their age. They may be a little closer to their true path in life. That was certainly our hope, and if it turns out to be true, it's worth a lot."

"This cannot be answered except by the children themselves. For us as parents the child's joy is all the benefit needed.

Today, our children have their own children and they also have chosen to unschool. Daily, they face a life that is entirely different from those things that came our way during their childhood."

"The peace, the joy, and the trust between us far exceeds anything I imagined possible in parent/child relationships. Seeing [my daughter] be who she is! Her self-confidence, her curiosity, the joy with which she lives are all strong characteristics that I think would have been damaged by school. Watching her engaged in the things that move her has been a lesson in and of itself for all the adults in her life—she is the most focused human being I've ever met. She can work for hours on something that is meaningful to her—nothing she wants is "hard" or "work" even, so my language isn't correct. (I'm sure if she were in school, though, she'd be labeled as having ADD)."

"My daughter's happiness, her curiosity, her love of exploration, her freedom. Our freedom as a family, the cooperative nature of our relationships and the trust between us that remains intact."

Reference

Gray, P., & Riley, G. (2013). The challenges and benefits of unschooling according to 232 families who have chosen that route. *Journal of Unschooling and Alternative Learning*, 7, 1-27.

6

What Leads Families to Unschool Their Children?

Report II from the Survey

Why 232 families chose to trust their children's educative instincts

MARCH 26, 2012

This is the second in a series of three reports on a survey of unschooling families that I conducted, along with Gina Riley, in the fall of 2011. The first report, described the survey method, gave some demographic information about the families that responded, and summarized their responses to questions about the definition and benefits of unschooling as applied to their family. My goal now, in Report II, is to describe the paths by which the families that responded to the survey came to unschooling. This report is based on a qualitative analysis that Gina and I conducted of the responses to Item six on the survey form, which reads as follows: Please describe the path by which your family came to the unschooling philosophy you now practice. In particular: (a) Did any specific school experiences of one or more of your children play a role? If so, briefly describe those experiences. (b) Did any particular author or authors play a role? If so, please name the author or authors and what most appealed to you about their writing. (c) Did you try homeschooling before unschooling? If so, what led you from one to the other?

Here, in brief, is what we found:

The Decision to Remove a Child (or Children) from School

In response to Question 6a, 101 of the 232 families indicated that at least one of their children attended school prior to starting unschooling and that the child's experience in school led them to remove the child from school. In their explanations, 38 of these families referred specifically to the rigidity of the school's rules or the authoritarian nature of the classroom as reason for removing the child; 32 referred to the wasted time, the paltry amount of learning that occurred, and/or to the child's boredom, loss of curiosity, or declining interest in learning; and 32 referred to their child's unhappiness, anxiety, or condition of being bullied.

Here, as illustration, is a representative sample of quotations from respondents' answers to Question 6a (names have been removed in each case):

Responses Emphasizing Rigidity of Rules and Authoritarian Nature of the Classroom

"The school principle threatened to have [my son] prosecuted for bringing a 'weapon' to school. The 'weapon' was a can of silly string."

"I saw kids punished for being inquisitive and talkative, which is something I thought most young kids were, naturally."

"We were increasingly frustrated by the way things were taught to the kids. One example: kids who understood things quickly in math still had to go through the tedious process of 'showing their work' even if they could figure it out in their heads. Our daughter was bored and frustrated with this kind of busy work. She was getting punished (loss of recess) for not doing her homework, yet got very good grades on her report card and a perfect score on her first MCAS exam."

"When my 5-year-old was going to be held back in kindergarten for not knowing his letters, I knew this was wrong and that all kids learn at a different pace."

"We were tired of our children being labeled and tired of them coming home exhausted and quite frankly full of nastiness. They weren't the nice people we remembered them to be. Once we brought them all home, they became 'people' again."

"Our oldest child, on her first day of school, was told that she must ask for permission to urinate and permission to eat. She told us that she was unwilling to do that, and we decided, with the school, to withdraw her after a few days of her leaving the school grounds and coming home."

Responses Emphasizing Boredom, Wasted Time, or Loss of Interest in Learning in School

"After I put them in public school for a time, it became extremely clear to me that being forced to follow someone else's idea of a curriculum was counterproductive, to the point of making them 'hate' learning (we found this intolerable)."

"We hated the blue ribbon public school our oldest attended. He had one hour of homework (reading comprehension and math worksheets) every night, for a 6-year-old! The work was too easy for him, and he hated it and dragged his feet every night, and we resented the intrusion into our family life and relaxing time."

"I worked in the classrooms a lot and saw a LOT of wasted time during which my kids were stuck sitting still and doing absolutely nothing."

"By fifth grade, when we took [our son] out, school was destroying his natural curiosity and love of learning. Too many hours in school and then working on homework. He said to me, 'Mom, when is my time?' It was breaking my heart."

"We found that increasing levels of homework and projects left us slaves to the school's schedule even after school hours and on weekends. Additionally, we found that our oldest child was losing his love of learning, and our second child did not have enough time for her passion and gift—the performing arts."

Responses Emphasizing the Child's Unhappiness, Anxiety, or Being Bullied at School

"School was awful for the whole family. Homework. Hours. Social issues. Lack of physical exercise. Lack of family time. Discipline problems. . . I was literally dragging my kids to school they hated it so much."

"My eldest son was late to read (late according to the school) and that frustration led me to explore other options, but I didn't pursue any at that time. Later when the same child was in third grade, the workload and his frustration level with it, while still achieving 'advanced' grades, seemed incongruous. He was working longer hours at school than his father spent at work. For what purpose?"

"My older daughter was having test anxiety (it was the first year that No Child Left Behind was implemented), wasn't eating at lunchtime, was overcome by the noise and smells, and was distracted in the classroom. My younger daughter was bored and beginning to refuse to participate in classroom activities. My older daughter had been unhappy her entire school career. I kept thinking she'd outgrow it, but she didn't. Things finally got to the breaking point and I pulled them out without having a plan, but knowing I could definitely do better than the school. I was done sending them someplace that made them so sad and created so much tension in our family."

"Our older daughter absolutely hated going to school and all of us were miserable. Due to misconceptions and lack of exposure to homeschooling (forget unschooling, even homeschooling is not common in India), we did not realize that it was a viable option, 'till desperation led us to consider it."

"The faculty repeatedly ignored situations where other kids attacked my son physically and verbally. And after two years of taking it, he pushed one of his bullies back and was suddenly in trouble (the bully was not in trouble even though his being a bully toward my son was witnessed by several teachers). The school repeatedly set my son up to fail and ignored my requests and demands for change. Then they called a meeting to discuss what to do 'about my son' instead of what they could to FOR HIM. . . I told them that there would be no such meeting."

"My eldest child lost her love of learning early on at school. Eventually she stopped even doing maths and went from top of the class to the bottom. This was due to a maths teacher who used to mock her and make her feel small."

"In the beginning of grade two, my daughter told me one evening about how one of her friends had been verbally threatened (the term used was 'YOU'RE DEAD MEAT') by another classmate, pushed up against a wall, and told that the classmate's older cousins were going to get her. I was appalled that this was happening to 8-year-olds and that, upon talking to my daughter's teacher about this incident, this type of inter-action was not considered alarming by the teaching staff. I never want my children to accept and numb themselves to think that treating other humans horrendously, unlovingly, and unkindly is normal! I wanted my children to know that a loving, more nurturing world exists, thus we began homeschooling!"

"When we first started homeschooling my oldest, at age 11, had been so emotionally damaged from his school experi-ences that we were shocked to see how quickly his personality rebounded within a month or two."

The Transition from Homeschooling to Unschooling

In response to Question 6c, 110 of the 232 families said they had tried homeschooling before transitioning to unschool-ing. As explanation for this transition, most of these families described the child's resistance to the home curriculum, the family's unhappiness by the stress the curriculum created, and/or the parents' observations that the child was learning more on his or her own initiative than through the imposed curriculum. Here is a representative sample of quotations il-lustrating these explanations:

"We did try school at home initially, using the Waldorf-inspired Oak Meadow curriculum. I think I was in love with the idea of 'playing school' like I was a little girl again! I loved ordering all the supplies and books and planning our 'lessons.' But each year, after a few weeks, I'd eventually start leafing through the pages trying to find content that was relevant, appealing, something that wouldn't make us both nod off! And when tears started flowing over math drills, I knew there had to be a better way. I started to question why it was necessary for my son to learn this thing at this time, and then realized, simply, that it wasn't."

"We came to unschooling from traditional homeschooling, because my then-5-year-old wholeheartedly rejected any attempts at regimentation. He learned twice as much if I simply strewed resources in his path and let him go. Unschooling is the only thing that works for him."

"With my oldest I had the entire school-at-home setup. I thought I had to do it that way for him to learn . . . We were both stressed and dreaded sitting down at the table for the day's lessons. Gradually, I started pulling back and began to see that the more I pulled back, the more he flourished. Eventually, we began to ditch curriculum and strict schedules until it evolved into unschooling."

"In the beginning we provided lots of exercise books, but our girl's reluctance to do them gradually led us to unschooling (anything looking like instructions made her run away and we didn't want this kind of relationship)."

"I never wanted to recreate school at home, but I did find that I pushed school-like activities on my kids in the transition time just after we left school. Eventually I saw with my own eyes and heart that anything my kids chose on their own was more meaningful, pleasant, and long-lasting than something I coerced them to do."

"It was terrible. We fought all the time and I found myself not only responsible for making him do his homework, but for teaching him as well. Too much pressure for both of us. We were both miserable."

"At first I tried Classical Method (The Well-Trained Mind) and reproduced school at home, complete with desk, worksheets, grades, etc. After a month, we were both miserable."

"We tried 'school at home' and it was a big flop—we were taking the problems that my son had at public school and were just changing the location. We tried a number of different styles of curriculum and they just didn't feel right. He and I were both happiest when I just let him be. In the meantime, I was researching all I could on different ways to homeschool and each time I read about unschooling I thought, 'That would work for him, I just know it would.' I was afraid to trust, though, so we muddled through pretending to homeschool. When my younger two children taught themselves to read, I had the ah-ha moment and said, 'Hey it really can work.'"

Other Factors Leading to the Unschooling Decision
Influential Authors

In response to Question 6b, the majority of respondents said that a particular author or authors did play a role in their decision to unschool. Not surprisingly, the author most often mentioned, by far, was John Holt (named by 127 respondents), the former teacher who went on to condemn forced schooling and promote Self-Directed Education in books such as *How Children Fail* and *How Children Learn*. Holt also coined the term *unschooling* and founded the first magazine devoted to unschooling, *Growing Without Schooling*. Holt's work continues to be carried on by Holt Associates, led by Patrick Farenga.

The next most frequently mentioned author was John Taylor Gatto (named by 52 respondents), the former New York State Teacher of the Year who left teaching because he was convinced that compulsory schools, no matter how one taught within them, were doing more harm than good. Gatto went on to write, among other things, *Dumbing Us Down: The Hidden Curriculum of Compulsory Schooling*; *A Different Kind of Teacher: Solving the Crisis of American Schooling*; and *Weapons of Mass Instruction: A Schoolteacher's Journey Through the Dark World of Compulsory Schooling*.

The third most often mentioned was Sandra Dodd (named by 39 respondents), who maintains a very active website devoted to unschooling and parenting, is author of *The Big Book of Unschooling*, and promotes a version of unschooling called "radical unschooling." Some of the respondents who mentioned Dodd were quite passionate about their respect for her ideas and influence.

Other authors mentioned with considerable frequency were Alfi Kohn, Grace Llewellen, Mary Griffith, Dayna Martin, Naomi Aldort, Ivan Illich, Jeanne Leidloff, Raymond & Dorothy Moore, Jan Hunt, Pat Farenga, Joyce Fetteroll, Rue Kream, and Susan Wise Bauer.

In addition to mentioning specific authors, many mentioned that unschooling websites, conferences, or lectures played a role in their decision. Many also mentioned the role of friends or acquaintances who were very successfully unschooling their children. [Editorial note: More than eight years have passed since this article was originally written. For updated information and new resources about unschooling and Self-Directed Education see the website of the Alliance for Self-Directed Education.]

The Decision to Unschool, Without an Intervening Period of Schooling

Eighty-six of the families who responded to the survey indicated that they chose unschooling right from the beginning, with no initial period of in-home or out-of-home school. Some of these said that they had made their decision even before they had any children, on the basis of their overall philosophy of life. At least a third of the 86 mentioned that their experiences with their young children, before school age, played a role in their decision to unschool. Some of these had been practicing "attachment" or "natural" parenting, and the decision to unschool seemed to follow naturally from that. For example, one mother wrote:

"My first child was a very high need infant, as Dr. William Sears calls babies who want to be in arms constantly. I learned to respond to her cues from day one and it was hard at first, giving up my old life! I learned about attachment parenting and implemented that brilliant idea into my life and followed her lead since. My home births for babies two and three propelled me with strength that I could also take control of my children's education, or really we could do it together, with them leading the way and me there to support them."

Nearly a third of the whole set of 232 respondents mentioned that their own negative school experiences influenced their decision to unschool their children, and many of these went directly to unschooling without any intervening period of schooling. For example, one in this group wrote:

"My own school experiences probably played a role. I discovered during my college experience that all of my schooling previous to college was completely unnecessary, and a waste of time . . . My K-12 experience was the unhappiest time of my life."

Some of the unschooling parents had been teachers or school counselors and made their decision to unschool based on those experiences. Here are two excerpts from parents in families in this category:

"My husband was teaching in a small high school in ___ by the time our oldest reached school age. I think the experience of dealing with kids who did not fit the system really opened his eyes. It pained him that so many students had simply given up all enthusiasm for learning at that point in their lives. The kids had either learned to jump through the hoops or had completely stopped trying, but there was very little real passion for learning left in them."

"I was a public school teacher. I loved teaching, for the most part. I loved being with the children. But I also began to see how flawed the system is, and when my children neared school age, I realized I didn't want them on the receiving end of all that was wrong."

And so, in sum, the people who responded to our questionnaire came to unschooling by many routes. Most often, it seems, the decision came from some combination of (a) a philosophy of life emphasizing the value of freedom and respect for individual differences; (b) observations of their children's learning and emotional experiences both inside and outside of schooling; (c) reflections on their own negative school experiences; and (d) knowledge gained from writers, speakers, websites, and the experiences of other unschooling families. In the next report in this series I will focus on the main challenges of unschooling for these 232 families.

7

The Challenges of Unschooling

Report III from the Survey

The biggest challenge to unschoolers is standing up to social norms

APRIL 11, 2012

This is the last in a series of three reports on the survey of 232 unschooling families that Gina Riley and I conducted in the fall of 2011. In the first report, I described the survey method, gave some demographic information about the families that responded, and summarized their responses to questions about the definition and benefits of unschooling as applied to their family. In the second report, I described the various paths that led these families to unschooling, including their previous experiences with conventional schooling and home-schooling, their observations of their children's natural ways of learning, and the influence of authors who had written about natural forms of education. Now, in this final report, I examine the challenges of unschooling as experienced by the families in the survey. This report is based on a qualitative analysis that Gina and I conducted of the responses to Question 7 on the survey form, which reads as follows: "What, for your family, have been the biggest challenges or hurdles to surmount in unschooling?" As a first step in the analysis, we coded the challenges that people described into several relatively distinct categories.

The category of challenges that contained the largest number of entries is the one that we labeled "Social Pressure." It includes negative judgments and criticism from others— including from relatives, friends, acquaintances, and even strangers—and perceived needs to justify their choice repeatedly to others. A total of 106 families (46 percent of the total) included this category of challenge in their answer to Question 7. In fact, for 57 of these families, Social Pressure was the only category of challenge listed.

The second largest category of challenges is the one that we labeled "Deschooling the Parent's Mind." This category has to do with parents' difficulties in overcoming their own, culturally ingrained "schoolish" ways of thinking about education. Included here are all descriptions of conflicts between the parent's unschooling philosophy and that same parent's ingrained, habitual ways of thinking and responding that could undermine that philosophy. A total of 95 families (41 percent of the total) included this category in their answer to Question 7. This category will become clearer, below, where I exemplify it with quotations. Many respondents cited challenges in both this category and the Social Pressure category, and some pointed to a link between the two. Others' criticisms would sometimes reawaken old, socially normative ways of thinking and raise again the fears that unschooling parents thought they had overcome, even when they could see full well that unschooling was working beautifully for their children. These fears could lead the parent to begin trying to direct and control their children's learning, which, if unchecked, would defeat the unschooling practice.

Both of these two most often mentioned categories of challenge have to do with the power of social norms. We are social creatures, and it is very difficult for us to behave in ways that run counter to what others perceive as normal. In the history of cultures, harmful normative practices or rituals may persist for centuries at least partly because of the stigma, or perceived stigma, associated with violating the norms. These have included such practices as foot binding in the upper classes in China and genital mutilation in many other cultures. Even people who knew that such practices were harmful performed them, because failure to do so would mark the family as "different" and therefore aberrant. School is the most predominant cultural ritual of our time. It is a practice ingrained as normal, even necessary, in the minds of the great majority of people. To counter it, one must overcome not just others' negative judgments, but also the judgments that rise up from one's own school-indoctrinated mind.

Other categories of challenge lagged well behind these first two in frequency. These remaining categories include: "Time/Career/Income" (problems deriving from a parent's inability to pursue a career, or earn more money, or have sufficient time for herself or himself while attending to the children at home), cited by 45 families; "Finding Friends" (problems of finding friends for their children to play with, or finding others who shared their philosophy), cited by 18 families; and "Legal Issues" (problems deriving from laws or regulations that make unschooling illegal or difficult to practice), cited by 15 families. Although "Legal Issues" was cited by only five percent families in North America, they were cited by 33 percent (5 out of 15) who resided in Europe.

The remainder of this post is devoted to selected quotations from the questionnaires, which illustrate each category of challenge that these unschooling families had to surmount.

Responses Illustrating Social Pressure as a Challenge

"By far the greatest challenge is with other people. It is such a radical concept, I think it feels so easy for people (especially family members) to criticize it. I get tired of feeling like I need to wait until my children are adults so I can finally say, 'See, it's all right!'"

"The biggest challenge has been overcoming fears about going against the norm and dealing with extended family members who are critical or unsupportive of our choices."

"We still have not told my husband's family that we are unschooling. We fear that they would panic and feel the need to step in. We don't want that tension for ourselves or our children."

"Answering the questions of other people who do not understand, including [those of] homeschoolers. Things like, what grade are you in, what curriculum do you use, how does an only child get any socialization, etc."

"I would say the only real challenge we have is dealing with others' (mostly strangers') prejudices and misunderstandings. When we say we homeschool (because 'unschooling' is met with blank stares most of the time) they assume I have little desks set up in my living room. They assume we have no social life. It just gets really, really tiring hearing those comments all the time (from people we meet out in public). Then a program comes on mainstream TV about unschooling and people think that is our life (these programs are usually sensationalized and edited in such a way as to portray us as neglectful, ignorant parents who don't care about their kids). I'm sick of answering questions like 'Well, that's fine for art and music, but what about math?' or 'How will your kids function in the Real World.' I don't always want to be an ambassador for unschooling, especially when I'm just trying to buy groceries! But it seems I often find myself in that situation and sometimes it is tiring."

"I think for us, being Christians, it is the stigma of being lazy parents. Unschooling is viewed as a hands-off approach to child rearing and is especially viewed as wrong or sinful in the Christian community. God loves order—or so it goes in their minds. The funny thing is that Jesus was probably unschooled."

"Our extended family was our biggest challenge. They were negative about homeschooling, and outraged by unschooling. We had to pull away from them for a little over a year. Now they see that [our daughter] is OK."

"My biggest hurdle has been gracefully handling interactions with friends and others who are invested in public school. I have a number of friends who are teachers or connected somehow with schools, and they saw (still sometimes see) what we do as thumbing our noses at them and their efforts."

"The skepticism and open disapproval of most of my friends and family was incredibly hard on me and isolated our family from our previous social group. I learned not to mention unschooling, because most of my old friends were already completely unsupportive of my decision to homeschool and the few people I told about unschooling completely freaked out."

"My daughter's father and stepmother were so opposed to it that they literally kicked her out of their house because they felt she was setting a bad example for their younger children."

"My MIL stopped asking about her grandchildren, unwilling to try to understand what we were doing or why. . .so they essentially lost a grandparent."

"When we first discovered unschooling, and really were exploring the philosophy, I was so excited to talk about it with family/friends. I learned very quickly that most people can't (won't?) understand, and some are downright disapproving. I have learned to talk about our unschooling in very schooly terms so that other people are more comfortable with us, and feel that we can relate on some level."

"Dealing with ignorant or defensive comments from those who don't know anything about unschooling is tiring."

"'Others', be they friends of friends, family members, or just people we have to interact with at public events or activities. . .. Questioning our children, interrogating us, having our motives challenged and scrutinized. Being accused of being selfish or of child neglect by not having them in a traditional school learning state standards. Occasionally, it breaks through and fills us with doubts and fears."

"The biggest hurdle has been other people. It is difficult to find others who are encouraging, especially people who live nearby. Our support has been conferences and online communities. . . . Others don't understand and look down on what we're doing. Most people are stuck in the school paradigm and feel it really is necessary for kids to go to school in order to be successful adults. They see things like bullying and doing work that has no meaning for you as necessary rites of passage to the 'real world,' which they see as boring, scary, and uninviting in general."

"We gave up discussing anything with family . . .Acquaintances and strangers used to bother us, until now that I have the proof that it works. . . . [But some] still try to think of something wrong, like how she missed the prom or doesn't act like a 'teenage girl'. It seemed to be somehow unusual in a bad way to have a mid-teen act like a graduate student, like maybe we had somehow been responsible for her being so 'different.'"

"My son hates explaining what we do or don't do at length to people who disapprove."

"Whenever you do something so outside the norm you have to practically become a spokesman for it. I'm not really interested in being the poster child for unschooling or putting my kids in that role, but it seems to be expected nonetheless."

Responses Illustrating Parents' Needs to Deschool Their Own Minds

"My son instinctually knows how to do this, but we [my husband and I] have had to unlearn a lot!"

"Something in us rebels at the thought of kids 'getting away' with not having to do math and spelling drills, homework, or having something forced upon them 'because they'll need it.' It's hard to see them spending so much time doing unstructured learning and having to fight the feeling that they're not learning effectively even when we can see that they are. In a way, we're actually jealous that they don't have to put up with the monotony, confusion, frustration, and 'socialization' (i.e. negative peer influence) that we had to deal with and can really focus on the joy of learning."

"The primary [challenge] is getting over my own worries that they aren't learning enough. I have to deschool myself constantly. There are so many messages in the media, and through family members (cousins, grandma, aunts) that my kids should know certain things on the school schedule. I have to remind myself constantly that they are always learning things, and that they have such a wonderful love of learning, and that they do not need to be on some else's schedule."

"Oh, keeping the status quo from invading my brain: 'TV is bad!' 'Computers are bad!' 'Children should be reading by age 5!' 'Video games make children violent!' It can be challenging to hear all this over and over and over again and not worry about it even though you can see perfectly well that none of these things are happening in real life."

"Coming from academia, probably the biggest hurdle was my own schooling or more accurately, deschooling myself and letting go of the belief that a 'good mom' provides endless 'educational' opportunities, without which a child is doomed to mediocrity. Learning to see learning everywhere, and understanding that learning has no connection to teaching."

"Refraining from pushing and coercing kids into things that I think are good for them. It never works out well and undermines the trust inherent in unschooling. At its root is worry that I've made a terrible mistake and they won't get what they need. Patently ridiculous, but the worry had a way of creeping in frequently in the early years. Not so much anymore as the benefits have become so clear as the girls have matured and proven very competent and eager learners."

"My own deschooling has been the biggest hurdle. Even though I have always wanted to focus on my kids' interests, I had a hard time letting go of the need to see hard proof (written work, projects, etc.) that they were learning."

"I still encounter little boxed up sections of my brain with old fears and assumptions. Right now [my son] is 6, and his friends are reading. I've found myself feeling anxious and unsure and then disgusted with myself for having those feelings. Now I'm learning to surf them—let them come up, remember that they're just outworn, fear-based reactions, let them subside, and watch how creatively [my son] navigates his world."

"I keep having to remind myself and get my husband to remind me that this is actually working. I was a teacher myself and this is just so not how I was taught at university to teach kids!"

"For me personally, getting over the feeling that I am not doing enough—those panicky moments when I jump in and try to force a bit of learning. I soon have regretted them, and now, day-by-day, I am amazed by what the children are learning — what they know."

"I have found that the biggest hurdles so far are all self inflicted. . .Sometimes it feels too easy and that there must be a catch. Am I just being lazy? For the love of God, what about the workbooks! Given our schooled background it is easy to believe that if it's 'educational', it can't be fun, and if it's fun (and easy), it can't be educational! I generally question the path we have chosen only because I do not know anyone who has homeschooled, let alone unschooled."

"I am definitely the biggest challenge! I have to get out of my way, a lot. Whether it is questioning whether their video game play is excessive to 'what about college?', sometimes just finding trust is hard! But I always eventually reason that a conversation with any of my children would allay the fears of even the most hardened skeptic; they are articulate, compassionate, engaged people, and I wouldn't change a thing about them or the path we've chosen (except maybe not having had to do the school thing first!)."

"Our own conditioning is the biggest challenge. The disapproval and criticism from family and friends is easier to deal with than the old tapes playing in our own heads."

Responses Illustrating the Time/ Career/Income Challenge

"Money money money money money. I have always had to work and sometimes more than others. Most of my at-home years were spent freelancing (I'm a writer) to close the gap, and then when my husband was laid off, I went full-time freelance with some on-site work. For one terrible, terrible year I worked full-time for a nonprofit—three days from home and two days on-site. It was very difficult and although my kids did OK, I about ran myself into the ground. . . .Plus my kids' social life depends on mine so much—it's one thing to drive them to events but being in the loop takes parental effort— and when I've been working I haven't been able to do that, which has meant they have missed out on some."

"The biggest challenge has been financial—so much to do and see and explore, not enough resources to do it all. But that too is part and parcel of living life and seeking options and alternatives to meet needs and desires and curiosities within the parameters of a single income household and the time away from home required for the working parent."

"Time—trying to balance work and 'parent alone time.'"

"Having time alone for me (mom) since my children are with me 24/7."

"Our biggest hurdle has just been fitting everything in, with so many children and different interests, allowing for each individual to follow his own path."

Responses Illustrating the Challenge of Finding Friends

"For us the main issues are the travel required for socializing—this can be tiring. We have to travel further to find girls my eldest daughter's age."

"Because our son is an only child, and the other children who live in our neighborhood attend school and then after-school care, we have had to make sure to provide plenty of opportunity for him to get together and play with other children, as he really enjoys being with other kids. Until we found a couple local(ish) unschooling/homeschooling networks with which we connected, it was challenging to find him children to play with as often as he wanted to get out and socialize . . .Also because my husband and I both work from home, it can be challenging during busy work weeks to balance everyone's schedules and needs to make sure everyone and everything is getting attention and support."

We live rurally, and it has been very challenging for the children to develop friendships with local people."

Responses Illustrating Legal Challenges

[From Finland, where even non-schooled kids must take tests.] "Especially when the official tests day at the local public school is approaching, we get more worried. Then we typically decline into the 'teacher-centered' mode and do our best to drill some test-taking-skills to him."

[From the UK] "The problems we have had are with the council and trying to make them realize it is a genuine educational philosophy. Also, I always panic every now and then in case they turn up and want 'evidence'."

[From France] "The fear of the inspection. In France, we're controlled each year, and it's a harsh time to defend the right we still have to educate according to a different pedagogy/philosophy from school."

[From France] "Education authorities, because we are controlled here by people who do not believe in homeschooling (so you could imagine what unschooling is for them). We are obliged to hide (so being outlaws) or to [compromise our unschooling principles]. . . . In the French law all 16-year-old children must have certain knowledge for each subject. So if you are doing totally unschooling it's impossible to be sure your child will attain this aim at sixteen."

[From North Carolina] "Currently, in our state, I have to give my child a standardized test once a year starting at age 7. I worry about this affecting my commitment to unschooling, since the state will be watching me."

[From New Hampshire] "Our biggest hurdles to unschooling have been our state's homeschool requirements. Although the NH requirements are easy and reasonable to comply with, there is still that burden hanging over us during the year that we 'should find a way to get some of this or that in the portfolio'. In fact, a couple of years ago my son and I rallied at the NH State House three times to prevent the passing of legislation that would have required all homeschoolers to take a standardized test in addition to the portfolio option! My son, who, on his own at age 14 began to write like crazy and subsequently wrote an entire book manuscript, wrote a letter to the newspaper recently stating how state requirements infringe upon his right to learn freely in the way that he wants to learn, because he is aware that he must cover certain 'subjects' whether he wants to or not."

Despite the challenges, none of the respondents expressed regret about their unschooling decision. For the many reasons for their lack of regret, look back at Reports I and II, for their descriptions of the benefits of unschooling and the experiences that led them to this path.

8

Survey of Grown Unschoolers I

Overview of Findings

Seventy-five unschooled adults report on their childhood and adult experiences

JUNE 7, 2014

In a study that preceded the one to be described here, Gina Riley (professor of education at Hunter College) and I surveyed parents in unschooling families—that is, in families where the children did not go to school and were not homeschooled in any curriculum-based way, but instead were allowed to take charge of their own education. In that study we asked questions about their reasons for unschooling, the pathways by which they came to unschooling, and the major benefits and challenges of that route of education. I posted the results of that study as a series of three articles on my *Psychology Today* blog (reprinted here as Essays 5, & 7). Gina and I also published an academic article on that study (Gray & Riley, 2013). [Editorial note: Gray and Riley have, since, also

published two academic articles on this survey of grown unschoolers (Gray & Riley, 2015; Riley & Gray, 2015).]

The respondents in that survey were very enthusiastic and
positive about their unschooling experiences. They described
benefits having to do with their children's psychological and
physical wellbeing, improved social lives, and improved ef-
ficiency of learning and attitudes about learning. They also
wrote about the increased family closeness and harmony, and
the family's freedom from having to follow a school-imposed
schedule. The challenges they described had to do primarily
with having to defend their unschooling practices to those
who did not understand them or disapproved of them, and
with overcoming some of their own culturally-ingrained, habitual ways of thinking about education.

The results of that survey led us to wonder how those
who are unschooled, as opposed to their parents, feel about
the unschooling experience. We also had questions about the
ability of grown unschoolers to pursue higher education, if
they chose to do so, and to find gainful and satisfying adult
employment. Those questions led us to the survey of grown
unschoolers that is described in this article and in three more
articles to follow.

Survey Method for Our Study
of Grown Unschoolers

On March 12, 2013, Gina and I posted on my *Psychology
Today* blog an announcement to recruit participants. That
announcement was also picked up by others and reposted on

various websites and circulated through online social media. To be sure that potential participants understood what we meant by "unschooling," we defined it in the announcement as follows:

"Unschooling is not schooling. Unschooling parents do not send their children to school and they do not do at home the kinds of things that are done at school. More specifically, they do not establish a curriculum for their children, do not require their children to do particular assignments for the purpose of education, and do not test their children to measure progress. Instead, they allow their children freedom to pursue their own interests and to learn, in their own ways, what they need to know to follow those interests. They may, in various ways, provide an environmental context and environmental support for the child's learning. In general, unschoolers see life and learning as one."

The announcement went on to state that participants must (a) be at least 18 years of age; (b) have been unschooled (by the above definition) for at least two years during what would have been their high school years; and (c) not have attended 11th and 12th grade at a high school.

The announcement included Gina's email address, with a request that potential participants contact her to receive a copy of the consent form and survey questionnaire. The survey included questions about the respondent's gender; date of birth; history of schooling, homeschooling, and unschooling (years in which they had done each); reasons for their unschooling (as they understood them); roles that their parents played in their education during their unschooling years; any formal higher education they had experienced subsequent to unschooling (including how they gained admission and how they adapted to it); their current employment; their social life growing up and now; the main advantages and disadvantages they experienced from their unschooling; and their judgment as to whether or not they would unschool their own children.

We received the completed questionnaires over a period of six months, and Gina and I, separately, read and reread them to generate a coding system, via qualitative analysis, for the purpose of categorizing the responses. After agreeing on a coding system, we then, separately, reread the responses to make our coding judgments, and then compared our separate sets of judgments and resolved discrepancies by discussion.

The Participants and Their Division into Three Groups

A total of 75 people who met the criteria filled out and returned the survey. Of these, 65 were from the United States, six were from Canada, three were from the UK, and one was from Germany (where unschooling is illegal). The median age of the respondents was 24, with a range from age 18 to 49. Eight were in their teens, 48 were in their 20s, 17 were in their 30s, and two were in their 40s. Fifty-eight (77 percent) were women, 16 were men, and one self-identified as gender queer. The high proportion of women probably represents a general tendency for women to be more responsive to survey requests than are men. It is not the case that more girls than boys are unschooled; indeed, our previous study, where parents were surveyed, there were somewhat more boys than girls undergoing unschooling in the families that responded.

For purposes of comparison, we divided the respondents into three groups on the basis of the last grade they had completed of schooling or homeschooling. Group I were entirely unschooled—no K-12 schooling at all and no homeschooling (the term "homeschooling" here and elsewhere in this report refers to schooling at home that is not unschooling). Group II had one or more years of schooling or homeschooling, but none beyond sixth grade; and Group III had one or more years of schooling or homeschooling beyond sixth grade. Thus, those in Group II could have had anywhere from one to seven years (K-6) of schooling/homeschooling and those in Group III could have had anywhere from one to 11 years (K-10) of schooling/homeschooling.

The table below shows the breakdown of some of our statistical findings across the three groups. The column headings show the number of participants in each group. The first three data rows show, respectively, the median and range of ages, the median and range of total years of schooling plus homeschooling, and the percentage of respondents that were female for each group. It is apparent that the three groups were quite similar in number of participants, median age, and percent female, but, of course, differed on the index of number of years of schooling plus homeschooling.

DATA SUMMARY (Based on preliminary analysis)

	I. No Schooling N = 24	II. No Schooling past 6th grade N = 27	III. Some schooling past 6th grade N = 24
Age: Mdn (range)	24 (18–35)	25 (19–37)	24.5 (18–49)
Years of schooling+hmschlng: Mdn (range)	0 (0–0)	5 (1–7)	8 (1–11)
Gender: % Female	19/24 = 79%	20/27 = 74%	19/24 = 79%
Some formal higher education	18/24 = 75%	23/27 = 85%	21/24 = 88%
Has or working on BA or higher	14/24 = 58%	12/27 = 44%	7/24 = 29%
Work matches childhood interests	21/24 = 88%	19/27 = 70%	18/24 = 75%
Financially Independent	11/15 = 73%	18/21 = 86%	14/19 = 74%
*Job/career in arts/ film/theatre/writing	19/24 = 79%	9/27 = 33%	8/24 = 33%
Evidence of entrepreneurship	15/24 = 63%	14/27 = 52%	11/24 = 46%

	I. No Schooling N = 24	II. No Schooling past 6th grade N = 27	III. Some schooling past 6th grade N = 24
Clear "yes" to unschool own child	18/23 = 78%	16/27 = 59%	16/24 = 67%
Clear "no" to unschool own child	1/23 = 4%	2/27 = 7%	2/24 = 8%

Statistically significant difference across groups.

Formal Higher Education after Unschooling

Question five of the survey read, "Please describe briefly any formal higher education you have experienced, such as community college/college/graduate school. How did you get into college without having a high school diploma? How did you adjust from being unschooled to being enrolled in a more formal type of educational experience? Please list any degrees you have obtained or degrees you are currently working toward."

I'll describe the responses to this question much more fully in the next article in this series, where I'll make ample use of the participants' own words. Here I'll simply summarize some of the statistical findings that came from our coding of the responses.

Overall, 62 (83 percent) of the participants reported that they had pursued some form of higher education. This included vocational training (such as culinary school) and community college courses as well as conventional bachelor's degree programs and graduate programs beyond that. As can be seen in data row four of the table, this percentage was rather similar across the three groups.

Overall, 33 (44 percent) of the participants had completed a bachelor's degree or higher or were currently full-time students in a bachelor's program. As shown in data row five of the table, the likelihood of pursuing a bachelor's degree or higher was inversely related to the amount of previous schooling. Those in the always-unschooled group were the most likely to go on to a bachelor's program, and those in the group that had some schooling past sixth grade were least likely to. This difference, though substantial, did not reach the conventional level of statistical significance (a chi square test revealed a $p = .126$). The colleges they attended were quite varied. They ranged from state universities (e.g. the University of South Carolina and UCLA) to an Ivy League university (Cornell) to a variety of small liberal arts colleges (e.g. Mt. Holyoke, Bennington, and Earlham).

Of the 33 who went on to a bachelor's degree programs, seven reported that they had previously received a general education diploma (GED) by taking the appropriate test, and three reported that they had gained a diploma through an online procedure. The others had gained admission to a bachelor's program with no high school diploma except, in a few cases, a self-made diploma that, we assume, had no official standing. Only seven of the 33 reported taking the SAT or ACT tests as a route to college admission, though the number taking one or the other of these tests could have been higher. By far, the most common stepping-stone to a four-year college for these young people was community college. Twenty-one of the 33 took community college courses before applying to a four-year college and used their community college transcript as a basis for admission. Some began to take such courses at a relatively young age (age 13 in one case, age 16 in typical cases) and in that way gained a head start on their college career. By transferring their credits, some reduced the number of semesters (and the tuition cost) required to complete a bachelor's degree. Several also mentioned interviews and portfolios as means to gain college admission.

The participants reported remarkably little difficulty academically in college. Students who had never previously been in a classroom or read a textbook found themselves getting straight As and earning honors, both in community college courses and in bachelor's programs. Apparently, the lack of an imposed curriculum had not deprived them of information or skills needed for college success. Most reported themselves to be at an academic advantage compared with their classmates, because they were not burned out by previous schooling, had learned as unschoolers to be self-directed and responsible, perceived it as their own choice to go to college, and were intent on making the most of what the college had to offer. A number of them reported disappointment with college social life. They had gone to college hoping to be immersed in an intellectually stimulating environment and, instead, found their fellow students to be more interested in frat parties and drinking. I will describe all this more fully in the next article in this series.

Employment and Careers

Question four of the survey read, "Are you currently employed? If so, what do you do? Does your current employment match any interests/activities you had as an unschooled child/teen? If so, please explain." Our analyses of responses to this question led us to generate a brief follow-up questionnaire, which we sent to all of the participants, in which we asked them to list and describe the paying jobs they had held, to indicate whether or not they earned enough to support themselves, and to describe any career aspirations they currently had in mind. Sixty-three (84 percent) of the participants responded to this follow-up questionnaire.

The great majority of respondents were gainfully employed at the time of the survey. Exceptions were some of the full-time students and some mothers with young children. Of those who responded to the follow-up questionnaire, 78 percent said they were financially self-sufficient, though some of these added that their income was modest and they were self-sufficient in part because of their frugal lifestyle. Several of them described frugality as a value and said they would far rather do work they enjoyed and found meaningful than other work that would be more lucrative. Collectively, the respondents had pursued a wide range of jobs and careers, but two generalizations jumped out at us in our qualitative analyses.

The first generalization is that a remarkably high percentage of the respondents were pursuing careers that we categorized as in the creative arts—a category that included fine arts, crafts, music, photography, film, and writing. Overall, 36 (48 percent) of the participants were pursuing such careers. Remarkably, as shown in data row eight of the table, 79 percent of those in the always-unschooled group were pursuing careers in this category. The observation that the always-unschooled participants were more likely to pursue careers in the creative arts than were the other participants was highly significant statistically ($p < .001$ by a chi square test).

The second generalization is that a high percentage of participants were entrepreneurs. Respondents were coded into this category if they had started their own business and were making a living at it or working toward making a living at it. This category overlapped considerably with the creative arts category, as many were in the business of selling their own creative products or services. Overall, by our coding, 40 (53 percent) of the respondents were entrepreneurs. As can be seen in data row nine of the table, this percentage, too, was greatest for those in the always-unschooled group (63 percent), but in this case the differences across groups did not approach statistical significance.

In response to the question about the relationship of their adult employment to their childhood interests and activities, 58 (77 percent) of the participants described a clear relationship. In many cases the relationship was direct. Artists, musicians, theater people, and the like had quite seamlessly turned childhood avocations into adult careers; and several outside of the arts likewise described natural evolutions from avocations to careers. As shown in data row six, the percentage exhibiting a close match between childhood interests and adult employment was highest for those in the always-unschooled group, though this difference did not approach statistical significance.

All of these generalizations regarding unschoolers' subsequent employment will be illustrated, with quotations from the surveys, in the third article in this series.

Respondents' Evaluations of Their Unschooling Experience

Question seven of the survey read, "What, for you, were the main advantages of unschooling? Please answer both in terms of how you felt as a child growing up and how you feel now, looking back at your experiences. In your view, how did unschooling help you in your transition toward adulthood?" In response to this, almost all of the respondents wrote about the freedom and independence that unschooling gave them and the time it gave them to discover and pursue their own interests. Seventy percent of them also said, in one way or another, that the experience enabled them to develop as highly self-motivated, self-directed individuals. Many also wrote about the learning opportunities that would not have been available if they had been in school, about their relatively seamless transition to adult life, and about the healthier (age-mixed) social life they experienced out of school contrasted with what they would have experienced in school.

Question eight read, "What, for you, were the main disadvantages of unschooling? Again, please answer both in terms of how you felt as a child growing up and how you feel now. In your view, did unschooling hinder you at all in your transition toward adulthood?" To this, 28 of the 75 respondents reported no disadvantage at all. Of the remaining 47, the most common disadvantages cited were (1) dealing with others' criticisms and judgments of unschooling (mentioned by at least 21 respondents); (2) some degree of social isolation (mentioned by 16 respondents), which came in part from there being relatively few other homeschoolers or unschoolers nearby; and (3) the social adjustment they had to make, in higher education, to the values and social styles of those who had been schooled all their lives (mentioned by 14 respondents).

For 72 of the 75 respondents, the advantages of unschooling clearly, in their own minds, outweighed the disadvantages. The opposite was true for only three of the participants, two of whom expressed emphatically negative views not just of their own unschooling, but of unschooling in general (to be detailed in the fourth article in this series).

Question nine read, "If you choose to have a family/children, do you think you will choose to unschool them? Why or why not?" One respondent omitted this question. Of the remaining 74, 50 (67 percent) responded in a way that we coded as clearly "yes." Within that group, eight already had children of school age and were unschooling them. Of the remainder, 19 responded in a way that we coded as "maybe" (for them it depended on such factors as the personality and desires of the child, the agreement of the other parent, or the availability or lack of availability of a good alternative school nearby), and five responded in a way that we coded as clearly "no." The five included two of the three who were negative about their own unschooling experience and three others, who, despite their positive feelings about their own unschooling, would, for reasons described in the final article in this series, not unschool their own child.

Limitation of the Survey

A major limitation of this study, of course, is that the participants are a self-selected sample, not a random sample, of grown unschoolers. As already noted, relatively few men responded to the survey. A bigger problem is that the sample may disproportionately represent those who are most pleased with their unschooling experiences and their subsequent lives. Indeed, it seems quite likely that those who are more pleased about their lives would be more eager to share their experiences, and therefore more likely to respond to the survey, than those who are less pleased. Therefore, this study, by itself, cannot be a basis for strong claims about the experiences and feelings of the whole population of unschoolers. What the study does unambiguously show, however, is that it is possible to take the unschooling route and then go on to a highly satisfying adult life. For the group who responded to our survey, unschooling appears to have been far more advantageous than disadvantageous in their pursuits of higher education, desired careers, and other meaningful life experiences.

The remaining three articles in this series will delve more deeply into these grown unschoolers' experiences, using their own words.

References

Gray, P, & Riley, G. (2013). The challenges and benefits of unschooling according to 232 families who have chosen that route. *Journal of Unschooling and Alternative Learning*, 7, 1-27.

Gray, P, & Riley, G. (2015). Grown unschoolers' evaluations of their unschooling experiences: Report I on a survey of 75 unschooled adults. *Other Education*, 4 (#2), 8-32.

Gina Riley, G., & Gray, P. (2015). Grown unschoolers' experiences with higher education and employment: Report II on a survey of 75 unschooled adults. *Other Education*, 4 (#2), 33-53, 2015.

9

Survey of Grown Unschoolers II

Going on to College

**What do grown unschoolers say about
their experiences with college?**

JUNE 17, 2019

A major concern of many families considering unschooling has to do with the question of whether or not it reduces the subsequent possibility of college. Unlike so many others in the general population, most unschoolers do not consider college admission, or college graduation, or high grades in college, to be in any general sense a measure of life success. Nor do I. Still, the concern about college is relevant. Many, if not most, potential unschoolers would be reluctant to take this self-directed route if it precluded the possibility of college and therefore the possibility of careers that at present more or less require college as a prerequisite. That is why we asked the grown unschoolers in our survey about their college experiences.

The objective conclusions from our questions about college were summarized in the first report in this survey. Briefly, we found that (a) 62 (83 percent) of the 75 respondents had pursued some form of higher education; (b) 33 (44 percent) had completed a bachelor's degree or were currently full-time students in a bachelor's program; (c) those who had been entirely unschooled (never schooled or homeschooled from K-12) were more likely to attend college than were those who had received some schooling or homeschooling; (d) many used community college as a stepping stone to a four-year college, and others went directly to a four-year college based on essays, portfolios, interviews, or other evidence of preparation; (e) their academic adjustment to college was generally quite smooth; (f) most felt advantaged in college because of their high self-motivation and capacity for self-direction; and (g) the most frequent complaints were about the lack of motivation and intellectual curiosity among their college classmates, the constricted social life of college, and, in a few cases, constraints imposed by the required curriculum or grading system.

The best way to convey the college experiences of the respondents is through their own words, so the rest of this article consists of quotations from the surveys. The quotations are selected, but are quite representative of the whole sample. To preserve anonymity, I have identified each only by gender, age at the time of filling out the questionnaire, and extent to which the person had been unschooled. I've also removed potentially identifying information from the quotations, especially the names of the colleges attended. The preponderance of women in the sample of quotations reflects the high ratio of women compared to men who responded to our survey (see the previous article). I have chosen quotations primarily from those who had the least schooling or homeschooling before college, and I've ordered them in such a way that those with no K-12 schooling or homeschooling are first.

Age 20, no K-12 schooling or homeschooling. This woman, though only 20 years old, had already earned a BA degree and had gained what, for her, was an ideal job in theatre production. She had taken some community college courses between age 13 and 16 and then transferred to a four-year BA program at her state university, which she completed in two and one-fourth years, graduating summa cum laude. She wrote, "It was not a rough adjustment for me. I found that because I had not been in school before attending college, I was much less burnt out than my peers and had a very fresh perspective. I learned basic academic skills (essay composition, research, etc.) very quickly. . . I struggled some with time management, but eventually developed a means of staying organized."

Age 21, no K-12 schooling or homeschooling. This young man was in his third year of a four-year BA program, majoring in philosophy at a selective Canadian university, about to declare honors status and with plans to pursue a master's in philosophy. In explaining how he was admitted, he wrote, "I set an appointment to talk with someone in the admissions department to find out what I would need to do to apply as an unschooler. After I talked briefly about myself, my achievements, and my style of education, and after he read a sample of my writing, he said 'I can't see any reason why you shouldn't be here', and proceeded to hand me the forms to become a student." Concerning adjustment, he wrote, "It was a bit hard to adjust to the amount of skimming-over that many introductory classes do: I can't bear it when ideas are left unexplored. Mainly because of the depth of the material covered, I've found that my best grades, and some of my best work, have come from 4000-level courses. I've always learned in a passionate way and don't want to stop the flow of an idea until it runs its course."

Age 24, no K-12 schooling or homeschooling. This woman, who had received a BA from a highly selective liberal arts college, wrote, "In contrast to [my classmates], I found great inspiration from my teachers. At [name of college redacted] the teachers must also be practitioners in their fields of study, so I was working with people who were actively interested and participating in their areas of expertise as a teacher and as an actor, writer, director, translator, and so on. Having someone with such a wealth of knowledge looking over my shoulder at the work I was doing was revolutionary. It was not something I wish I had earlier, not something I felt had been lacking my whole life, but it was something that inspired me for my four years at school." At one point in her college career this young woman was asked to lead a meeting of students in order to provide feedback to the instructor of a course. She wrote, "I discovered that people wanted the teacher to tell them what to think. 'I wish he'd told us what to think when we read *Macbeth*' someone said. 'I wish he'd let us know what he wanted us to do in our *Hearts of Darkness* essays' and on and on. It had never, ever occurred to me to ask someone else to tell me what to think when I read something." This respondent also wrote that the biggest drawback to college, for her, was the lack of a normal, age-mixed social life—with people who are not all students. To achieve that, she joined the local Unitarian Universalist church where she served as religious educator while still a student.

Age 24, no K-12 schooling or homeschooling. This woman, who was currently a full-time student working for a master's degree in English, wrote: "I began attending a community college when I was 16 and enjoyed every second of it. I did not feel as though I had to adjust to anything. After my first psychology class, which was the first time I had to take notes during a class, I went right home and began typing and organizing my notes. I continued going part-time for two years until I was 18. The community college accepted my diploma, which I created myself and my parents signed, along with my transcript, which I also created. I turned my interests and activities into 'courses' for the transcript and included a list of books that I had read over the last 4 years. When I began looking for a four-year university to transfer to, my decision not to take the SATs had a minor effect on my choices for schools. One school refused to even open my application without SAT scores, even though I had written them a letter detailing my success at the college level for the last three years. I chose a university that allowed me to register as a part-time student for my first semester and then transfer into a full-time program without having to provide SAT scores."

Age 29, no K-12 schooling or homeschooling. This woman, who had graduated with high honors from a selective private women's college and then gone on to a master's degree, wrote, "On top of accepting me, they put me into their freshman honors class. I definitely felt strange going into a formal school, especially being in an honors program. I spent long hours studying and doing my homework—way more work than my classmates were doing. After I got straight As for the first half of my first semester, I started to relax a little more, and I realized I was working way too hard. So I learned how to learn like my fellow classmates were—by memorizing everything just before a test. I still kept getting straight As but was doing hardly any work at all. Eventually I learned how to balance it—actually delving into material I enjoyed and memorizing the stuff I wasn't interested in. It wasn't hard; it mostly just made me really appreciate the fact that I hadn't been in school my whole life. . . I definitely experienced a [social] transition in college. I wasn't into frat parties, drinking heavily and the like, so my first year/first two years I was a bit of a loner, with only a few friends. My last year in school I finally started drinking and going to house parties, so I 'fit in' a little better and got a wider group of 'friends.' I realized this was how everyone else in college was socializing and it felt off to me, not genuine or a way to really make lasting connections. Outside of school I returned to how I had always

functioned socially, and lo and behold, that was what everyone else outside of school was doing. I met friends through
my jobs, through theatres I worked in, through other friends,
and at coffee shops."

Age 29, no K-12 schooling or homeschooling. This woman,
who had earned a bachelor's degree in fine arts, wrote, "I
did have a high school diploma. Despite the completely unschooled nature of my upbringing, my mother had our home
registered as a private school with the state of CA, so on paper
I looked 'normal' in the system. . . I went to community college part-time between the ages of 16 and 19. I transferred to
a four-year school, which I attended for three years before receiving my BFA with High Distinction at 22 years old. I loved
college—it stands out as one of the most focused and fulfilling
periods of my young life! When I began community college,
I was younger than other students, and I was concerned that
I would be behind, but I wasn't. I didn't like taking tests, and
I still feel a lot of anxiety about tests, but I excelled in most
ways and graduated with a high GPA."

Age 30, no K-12 schooling or homeschooling. This man took
classes at a local state college beginning at age 16, and then
transferred to a small, selective, progressive private college
where he completed a BS in conservation biology and ecology.
After that, he earned an MS at a state university and completed one year of a Ph.D. program at another state university,
before taking a leave of absence because of a serious illness.
Concerning adjustment, he reported no difficulty with the
academic work, but objected to the constraints imposed by

the system of evaluation. He wrote, "Even the requirement-free environment of [name of college redacted] felt stifling to me (e.g. its perverse grading incentive to avoid one's own directions within a field in favor of the professor's predilections, formal academic bias to the near exclusion of experiential learning, and emphasis on tangible academic products rather than learning/applying process), and grad school has been many times worse (not only in terms of more structured and formalized educational paradigms, but also of lower-level educational opportunities)." He nevertheless plans to return to the Ph.D. program when his illness is controlled, as he is committed to a career aimed at restoring and maintaining biodiversity.

Age 32, no K-12 schooling or homeschooling. This woman, now a mom on the brink of unschooling her own children, wrote: "I took a course in Emergency Medicine and worked a couple of odd jobs while I researched college options, selected my preferred school, and went about the application process. I received a scholarship for a large chunk of my undergraduate education due to a portfolio that I assembled and my college interviews. Applying for college didn't seem to be too difficult without an official diploma, because I had SAT scores to submit and high school transcripts that my mom prepared from all of her years of journaling my unschooling exploits. I remember being very restless for the first one to two years of college. I didn't feel very challenged by the core classes and was itching to move on to my major and minor classes. College was fun, but I was stunned to realize that the majority of

the other students didn't work or pursue any other areas of
their lives apart from their studies and partying. I supported
myself throughout my four-year degree, typically working at
least two jobs while taking well above the minimum class/
load requirements so that I could graduate on time. Two years
into my degree I took a full-time job in the creative department of the local newspaper, where I continued to work after
graduation."

Age 35, no K-12 schooling or homeschooling. This woman,
who had earned a BA at a small progressive college and then
a master's degree, wrote, "Through my whole college experience I balked at students who didn't do the work, even in
the courses that were less than desirable or exciting for me.
I think my educational background set me up for thinking
'why are you there if you aren't going to participate?' This was
frustrating for me to see. For I have always chosen, myself,
to pursue education, and even though this personal choice
meant that there were some courses I had to take that I wasn't
excited about, I still knew what my motivation was for being
there. Over time I have learned that these fellow students who
were frustrating to be around had been exposed to a drasti-
cally different relationship with learning and education."

*Age 19, no K-12 schooling or homeschooling past second
grade.* This young woman had been diagnosed with dyslexia
when she was in second grade at school and was taken out of
school because of her unhappiness there. As an unschooler, she
learned to read at her own pace and in her own way. She was
also diagnosed with other learning disabilities, but found ways

to overcome them. During her last two years of unschooling, she took community college courses and then transferred to a bachelor's degree program at a selective private liberal arts college. She wrote, "I enrolled at [name of college redacted], where I just completed my freshman year. I maintained a 3.9 GPA through the whole year, and I am returning there in the fall . . . I think that unschooling actually prepared me better for college than most of my peers because I already had a wealth of experience with self-directed study. I knew how to motivate myself, manage my time, and complete assignments without the structure that most traditional students are accustomed to. While most of my peers were floundering and unable to meet deadlines, I remained on top of my work because I have always been an independent learner. I know how to figure things out for myself and how to get help when I need it. While I struggled to adjust in the beginning, it was purely due to the difficulties caused by my learning disabilities. By the end of the year I had overcome my struggles and excelled in school. I am currently working on my BA in English, and after that I intend to go on for a master's in library science."

Age 24, no K-12 schooling or homeschooling past second grade. This man, unlike most of the other respondents, reported that he had to jump through some hoops to get into community college, as a stepping-stone to a bachelor's program at a selective state university, but had no difficulties adapting academically. He wrote, "At first I did not want to attend college. When I graduated from homeschooling/unschooling, I worked at a gym selling gym memberships for two years. Ultimately, I figured out that I needed to go to college so I attended a local community college. It was difficult getting in without a high school diploma, and I had to go to the county school board office to obtain a 'homeschool completion affidavit' to prove to the college that I finished the 12thgrade. After a bunch of red tape, they accepted it. Since I never took the SAT, ACT or other standardized test for college prior to enrolling in the community college, I had to take a placement test before I could enroll in classes. After all of this was out of the way, I was viewed as a regular student. I went on to graduate from the community college with an associate's degree and a 4.00 GPA. Then I attended [name of university redacted] and obtained a bachelor's degree, also with a 4.00 GPA. Most recently, I just finished my master's degree at [name of university redacted]."

Age 24, no K-12 schooling or homeschooling past second grade. This woman, who earned a BA from a large state university, wrote, "There is an adjustment period going into 'school' from unschooling, but you also have the huge advantage of not being burned out and hating school already. Learning is still something you look forward to." This respondent went on to say that she received nearly all As and then a full scholarship to law school, and added: "I'm not trying to brag, so much as prove that unschooling works. We took a lot of crap from friends, relatives, and strangers during the entire time we were unschooling. So now, I like having the credentials to prove that unschooling is a legitimate way to educate and indeed, in my book, the preferred way."

Age 26, no K-12 schooling or homeschooling past second grade. This woman, who had graduated with honors from a highly selective liberal arts college, wrote, "The transition was a difficult one for me, not for the academics, but for the feeling of being trapped within a system. The college bubble felt tiny to me and I was in a constant state of simmering frustration at being told even simple things like which classes to take and when. As someone who had made those choices myself for years, I felt disrespected that it was assumed that I didn't know what level of study I was ready for. It took most of the first year for me to come to a place of acceptance, remembering that this, too, was a choice that I made that I could change if I wanted to. I never loved college like many people do and never felt as free as I had before college or in the time after I graduated." This respondent subsequently attended graduate school in a medical related field and reported that to be a better experience because of the real-world setting of the clinical work.

Age 35, no K-12 schooling or homeschooling past fourth grade. This woman, who had gained a degree from a highly selective liberal arts college, wrote, "I applied to eight colleges and was accepted at all of them. . . I interviewed at all eight colleges; for most of them I was their first 'homeschool/unschooled' applicant. Several colleges told me I was accepted at the conclusion of the interviews, right after they informed me that I was 'surprisingly' well-spoken and bright. I did take (and did very well on) both the SAT and the ACT, which probably offset the lack of transcripts. . . The transition was fairly easy, though I was homesick. I think college is a lot like unschooling—you take classes that interest you, do most of the work on your own, and are responsible for getting it done and turned in on time. You are really responsible for your own education! I received a BA in both computer science and mathematics. It proves something: I never had any formal math training beyond fifth grade, but ended up tutoring other students in Calculus 1, 2 and 3. I never had a computer of my own until my junior year of college, but majored in computer science where I wrote extensive computer programs, and pro-grammed my own robot." This person then went on to a BS and master's in nursing, became a nurse practitioner, and, at the time of the survey, was contemplating going back to school for a doctorate.

Age 32, no K-12 schooling or homeschooling past seventh grade. This woman, who had received a bachelor's degree from an Ivy League university, was a mother unschooling her own children, a yoga instructor, and a student training to do yoga therapy when she filled out the survey. Concerning college admission and adjustment to college, she wrote, "When I was 15, I wanted to take community college courses. At that time, dual enrollment of homeschooled students wasn't really accepted, so I was told I needed to get a GED to be allowed to enroll. Although I think it disappointed my parents for me to get my GED, it has helped to have that paper that shows I completed some sort of high school education. That said, I refuse to take standardized tests now (because I believe they aren't a measure of intelligence or even what a student has learned), so I did complete my associate's degree before I attempted to transfer to a four-year university (some schools will accept a two-year degree in place of SAT/ACT scores). I graduated from the university with a BA in psychology. I think unschooling helped me adjust to college; I was so used to being able to study whatever I wanted that it seemed natural to take classes that interested me. And unschooling also follows the premise that if a child has a goal, they'll learn whatever they need to in order to meet it."

Before closing, it's worth noting that we also found that those who did not pursue higher education reported that they did not need it to learn what they wanted to know or to pursue their chosen careers. For example, one wrote, "I've continued to unschool into adulthood and will continue throughout my life. I think internships and apprenticeships would be the natural extension of unschooling into the traditional workplace. If I become interested in a field that seems like college would be a good resource for, I would look into it—but I would still consider it part of the unschooling journey, which for me simply means following curiosity wherever it leads." Another stated simply, "As an adult, I realize that unschooling helped me see that college wasn't necessary to have a successful, fulfilling life."

As I noted in the first article on this survey, we must be cautious in interpreting the findings. By necessity, the sample here is a group of grown unschoolers who chose to participate, and they may well be among those unschoolers who are happiest with their experiences and most eager to tell about them. However, at minimum, we can conclude this: The college option is very definitely available to unschoolers. Those who want to go to college and take the steps required to get in seem to have no particular difficulty getting in or doing well once there. Moreover, the similarities in responses within this relatively diverse sample suggests a certain common ground of experience. The grown unschoolers who went on to college had good reasons in their own minds for doing so, did not want to waste their time there, seemed to work harder and achieve more than did their schooled classmates, and generally felt advantaged because of their previous experiences controlling their own lives and learning.

10

Survey of Grown Unschoolers III

Pursuing Careers

When people opt out of K-12 schooling,
what sorts of careers do they go on to?

JUNE 21, 2014

This is the third in a series of four posts describing the results of a survey of grown unschoolers that Gina Riley and I conducted. It is about the career choices of people who skipped all or part of K-12 and took charge of their own education. Before reading on, you may want to look back at the first article in this series. It presents the definition of unschooling that served as a criterion for admission into the study, describes our survey method and ways of analyzing the findings, presents age and gender breakdowns of the 75 grown unschoolers who were included, classifies them into three groups based on amount of unschooling, and presents a breakdown of some of the statistical findings according to those groups.

Now, in this third article in the series, I elaborate—beyond the statistical summary presented in the first post—on the careers that these generally young adults (median age 24) have pursued. The information presented here came primarily from Question four of the survey, which read, "Are you currently employed? If so, what do you do? Does your current employment match any interests/activities you had as an unschooled child/teen? If so, please explain." Further information also came from a brief follow-up questionnaire in which we asked them to list and describe the paying jobs they had held, to indicate whether or not they earned enough to support themselves, and to describe any career aspirations they currently had in mind. As noted in the first post, the great majority were gainfully employed and self-supporting, despite the difficult economic time in which the survey was conducted. In what follows I will elaborate, with quotations from the respondents' survey forms, on five general conclusions regarding careers that emerged from our qualitative analyses, namely (1) many chose careers that were extensions of their childhood interests, and (2) they typically chose enjoyable and meaningful careers over potentially more lucrative ones; (3) a high percentage chose careers in the creative arts; (4) a high percentage were entrepreneurs; and (5) a high percentage, especially of the men, chose STEM careers.

Careers as Extensions of Childhood Interests

By our coding, 58 (77 percent) of the 75 participants described a clear relationship between their childhood interests and their current vocation or career. This percentage was highest for the 24 participants in the always-unschooled group (21/24

= 88 percent), but was high in the other two groups as well (see the table in the first article in this series). The sample included professional artists and musicians who had played at art or music as children; computer technicians and programmers who had developed their skills in childhood play; and outdoor enthusiasts who had found ways to make a living that embraced their love of nature. Here are four examples that are among my favorites—favorites because they are the kinds of careers that school curricula ignore, careers that can strike the fancy of brave young people not in school, who have time and freedom to discover their passions and follow them.

Circus performer, circus entrepreneur, and tall ship bosun. One of our respondents, a 26-year-old woman who had always been unschooled, wrote: "At the age of 3, I decided to become a circus performer, and at the age of 5, I enrolled in an after-school circus program. I trained and performed as a circus performer continuously until the age of 17 and on-and-off ever since. From the ages of 19 to 24, my best friend and I ran our own contemporary circus company. As a result of that, I overcame a strong fear of heights to work as a trapeze artist and learned a considerable amount about rigging so that I would be able to ensure my own safety in the air. . . As my circus career has waned, I've tried a number of new things and the one that caught my full attention has been tall ship sailing. Working on the ocean is a very captivating experience and it employs the skills that I learned in the circus nearly every single day—skills like balance, hand-eye coordination, and even getting along with people in cramped living arrangements. I am currently employed as a tall-ship rigger/bosun. The job of bosun can change from ship to ship, but aboard training vessels my work involves maintenance as well as training and sailing. I am in charge of inspecting, maintaining and fixing the rigging, the sails, the deck and the hull. Additionally, I am expected to be involved in sailing the vessel, leading a watch during extended periods at sea, educating the public about the history of the vessels and educating the trainees about sail handling and vessel maintenance. . . I would like to sail large sailing vessels around the world. I am currently studying for a 100T master's license from the US Coast Guard that would allow me to be the captain of a vessel of 100 gross tonnes or less. USCG license are graduated by size of vessel and area of operation so this is the first step towards a license for a larger vessel."

Wilderness aerial photographer. This 21-year-old man, who left school after first grade, had started a business of taking beautiful (I can say that, because I saw some of them) artistic photos of wilderness scenes from the air. He wrote: "Growing up with so much freedom was awesome! I did lots of outdoor activities including skiing in the winter and hiking/camping in the summer. If I hadn't done it this way, I'm not sure I would have been able to combine the three things I really enjoy—outdoors, flying, and photography—into a business." He wrote further that he started his own photography business when he was 15 years old and also, that same year, started paragliding. The paragliding led to an interest in flying fixed-wing aircraft, and then he combined all three of his passions into a single business.

Assistant (beginning at age 18) to a famous movie director, producer, and screenwriter. This young man, who was 20 years old when he responded to the survey, was unschooled except for kindergarten and ninth grade (he went to school for ninth grade to "try it out"—he made honor roll and then left). His passion for film started early. By age 11 he was making You-Tube videos with friends. He began taking community college courses in mass communication at age 16, and, at age 18, was in the process of applying to film school when a great opportunity arose—to be a local production assistant on a major film that was being produced where he lived. His bosses liked him so much that they told him, "If you can get yourself to L.A., we'll keep you on the show." One thing led to another, he became close to the famous director, and at the time of the survey had a higher-level job, in L.A., on the production side of another major film. In response to our question about whether he earned enough to be financially independent, he wrote, "very much so." His ultimate goal is to direct movies himself, and he is working diligently toward that goal.

Self-employed polymath. A number of respondents showed a readiness, even eagerness, to change careers as their interests changed—just as they had changed activities as their interests changed when they were children. The extreme of this was one of the older respondents to our survey, age 39 at the time. He had experienced a mix of schooling and unschooling through 10th grade and then left high school for good. He went on to earn a bachelor's degree in mechanical engineering and a career identity that he refers to as "self-employed polymath." He wrote, "As a polymath, what I do now is very much what I have always done (I mostly ignored traditional schooling, even when I was forced to go); I do anything and everything that catches my attention. Life is about learning, growing, and sharing your discoveries with others who want to learn and grow, too." His list of jobs held over the years includes, but is not limited to, the following: research & development consultant for a medical manufacturing company; clinical hypnotherapist; master practitioner of neurolinguistic programming; director of tutoring services for a community college; wilderness survival, first aid, and bushcraft expert; PADI dive master instructor (scuba diving); martial arts instructor (Kung Fu, Judo, and Jeet Kun Do); and author of two published children's books (and currently working on a new series of bedtime stories).

Enjoyable and Meaningful Careers over Potentially More Lucrative Ones

This generalization overlaps considerably with the previous one, about careers as extensions of childhood interests. Unschooled children play, explore, and observe in the real world and in that way develop interests and abilities that can become pathways to careers. Several of our respondents said that their life as adults was not much different from their earlier life as unschoolers, as they continued to play, explore, and learn. In response to our question about whether they were financially independent, many said that they could support themselves only because they lived frugally, but they would rather live frugally and pursue their interests than make more money at a job that didn't interest them.

The four case examples above illustrate this second generalization—about pursuing enjoyable and meaningful careers—as much as they do the first generalization. Here are three more examples, however, in which the career reflects not so much the specific activities of childhood, as a set of ideals or social concerns that began to take root in childhood.

Greenpeace activist and community organizer. This woman, age 28 at the time of the survey, was one of the more schooled participants in the survey. She attended public school through age 13 and then refused to go anymore, and so was unschooled after that. As a child she immersed herself in art, but she was also interested in "revolutions and wildlife." I suspect that her school refusal was itself a sign of her revolutionary spirit. She went to art college, with the support of a substantial scholarship awarded on the basis of her portfolio, and subsequently taught art for several years. But then she shifted careers to her other great interest and became a full-time Greenpeace activist, fundraiser, and manager. In response to our question about supporting herself financially, she wrote: "Yep, I make a modest salary. I didn't exactly choose my job because it's the highest paying. It's more important to me that I spend my time doing something that benefits my community."

Founder of an environmentally and socially responsible construction company. This woman, age 30 at the time of the survey, had never gone to school but was homeschooled up to age "13 or 14," when full unschooling began. She wrote: "I am an owner/employee of a construction company. . . The company is a direct reflection of many of my interests and activities as an unschooled youth. For example, democracy in the workplace, environmental stewardship, construction and building, facilitation and project management. . . I am also the president of a small non-profit that works to support the use of alternative materials in construction through the development of technical guidelines. I am the project manager for our technical guideline project and coordinate with our diverse teams of supporters around the world. My interest in regulation and policy development, as well as a commitment to support the use of environmentally friendly alternative materials, are both directly connected to interests and projects I undertook as an unschooled young adult. . . I completed a series of internships over 3 years, during which I studied permaculture, natural building, community facilitation, and conflict resolution. The main advantage of unschooling was that it supported me in understanding myself clearly, and helping me craft an adult life that is meaningful to me. I do not identify as ever having stopped unschooling—I am continuing to learn as much as I did as a youth. When I was 15, I was studying microscopes and nuclear particles, and now I am studying non-profit bylaws and building codes, or training for a marathon. I am 30 years old, and I have been practicing how to run my life, be motivated towards my own goals, think creatively about how to solve problems, and seek out what interests me for 20 years. I find myself consistently in an advantageous position compared to my 'schooled' peers."

Urban planner, with focus on non-motorized transportation design. This 30-year-old person, who was entirely unschooled from K-12, self-identified as gender queer and preferred not to be classed as either male or female (so I'll use the pronoun they). After completing a bachelor's degree program, they held jobs that reflected their interests in planning, management, and urban development. These included assistant town planner in a small city, administrative assistant for a public health department at an Ivy League university; research assistant for a project involving bicycle transportation (while a graduate student); program coordinator for a low-income housing non-profit; and post-graduate research fellow for the Bureau of Transportation in a large city. They wrote: "My goal is to build a career in either bicycle and pedestrian transportation planning/policy or in human factors engineering... My interests have typically come in short, intense cycles. I figured this out when I was about 16 and started researching career options that would let me change projects every few months. At 17 I discovered urban design, which has acted as a thematic connection for a lot of my more passing interests over the last decade. As a topic, it connects to some of the things I enjoyed as a teenager—theater set design, model building, textile design, ecology—but it took moving from the rural areas where I grew up to [large city name redacted] before I really understood what it was that interested me about design. My path since then has been twisty but generally linear. I studied pre-architecture and drafting at community college, got into architecture and urban design at college, wrote a thesis on post-socialist urban planning policy in Vietnam and

Hungary in undergrad, worked in a town planning office for a while, and got interested in my current specialties of non-motorized transportation and qualitative research methods for analyzing travel behavior once I started grad school."

Careers in Creative Arts

As I noted in the first post, by our coding, 36 (48 percent) of the 75 survey participants were pursuing careers that we categorized as in the creative arts, defined broadly as including fine arts, crafts, photography, film, theater, and writing, and those in the always-unschooled group were especially likely to be pursuing such careers. The aerial nature photographer and assistant movie producer, described earlier as examples of continuity between childhood passions and adult careers, are also examples of careers in the creative arts. Here are three more examples:

Production manager at a large theater company. This 29-year-old woman, who was unschooled for all of K-12 but had gone on to a bachelor's degree in theatre arts, wrote: "I am a working artist and the production manager of [major theater company in New York redacted]. I feel like the way I was raised led directly to what I do now. The tools I learned as a child—to pursue new ideas/interests/knowledge, to creatively solve problems, to actively participate in my community, and more—have helped me greatly. It's actually pretty much what I still do, just in the context of a grown-up life. The organizing, lighting design, dancing, making things, is exactly what I was doing as a child and teen." To our question about financial independence, she wrote: "NYC is a hard city to live in, but I have been financially independent the whole time since graduating from college in 2008. I have never had trouble finding work. I gravitate to experimental performance and work with/for a lot of artists. My fees are not high. But it's worth it to me to work on projects that I find interesting and believe in."

Textile artist/crafter and entrepreneur. This 21-year-old woman, who was unschooled for all of K-12 and had pursued no higher education, wrote: "I'm a self-employed artist/crafter, I sell online and locally. I am absolutely doing what I was interested in as a child! I've always been making things; I love what I do." In response to our question about financial independence, she wrote: "Yes I became financially independent at age 19 and have maintained that. It is very important to me to make a good living and I feel very proud watching my income rise little by little each year. As an unschooled adult I felt pressured to succeed professionally because people doubted I could/would, and also to show my younger siblings what that looks like for us."

Self-employed piano and violin instructor and aspiring performer. This 28-year-old woman, who was homeschooled to age 10 and unschooled after that, had two jobs at the time she responded to the survey. One was that of self-employed web designer, a business she had maintained for about 10 years. The other—and more significant job to her—was that of self-employed piano and violin instructor, which she had been doing for about seven years. Concerning the latter, she wrote: "This is my career path, and I have built it all myself. I currently have 31 students. I teach one-on-one private lessons, teaching pieces/songs, theory, ear training, music history, composition, technique, performance, and sharing my passion for music. I love my job!" In response to our question about financial independence, she wrote: "Yes. I run my own business, and it brings in enough income to comfortably sustain a living in the expensive area of [name of city redacted]. 'Making a good living' is very important to me. But the way I look at making a good living is as follows: Being financially responsible for my own life and affording the things that are important to me. And most important, doing this in a way that brings me joy." At the conclusion of her response, she added, "I love my current career as a music teacher, but I am also aspiring to perform with my band as a second career path. I play bass and sing in this band, and next week we are heading in to the studio to record a full-length album that we raised the money for through a Kickstarter campaign. We are continuing to work toward our goals with this record, making touring plans for the coming year, and looking over an offer from a record label."

Entrepreneurship

As noted in the first article in the series, respondents were coded as being entrepreneurs if they had started their own business and were making a living at it or working toward making a living at it. This category overlapped considerably with the creative arts category, as many were in the business of selling their own creative arts or services. Overall, by our coding, 40 (53 percent) of the respondents were entrepreneurs.

Sociologists who have studied work satisfaction have found that the kinds of jobs and careers that people find most satisfying are those that involve a great deal of occupational self-direction. One thing that is eminently clear from our survey is that the unschoolers who responded had, overwhelmingly, chosen careers very high in this quality. They were, by and large, working for themselves or in work environments where they were their own bosses. No big surprise here: People who opted out of top-down schooling, where they would be the underlings doing work dictated to them by others, generally opted out of that in their careers also. I won't provide new case examples here, as more than half of the case examples I've already described were entrepreneurs.

STEM Careers

We had not initially thought of coding the careers to see how many were in the STEM (science, technology, engineering, and math) category, but did so after the question was raised by a reader of the first article in this series when it was posted on my *Psychology Today* blog. We used the definition of STEM published by the National Science Foundation, which includes social sciences as well as natural sciences, technology, engineering, and math. However, we only included people in the social sciences if they were conducting research in that realm and/or were doing applied work that made use of technical aspects of a social science. As we did with other analyses, Gina and I first coded independently and then compared notes and resolved differences in discussion.

Overall, by our coding, 22 (29 percent) of the 75 participants were pursuing STEM careers. When we broke this down by gender (leaving out the person who did not wish to be classified by gender), we found that 13 (22 percent) of the 58 women and eight (50 percent) of the 16 men in the sample were coded as having STEM careers. Despite the relatively small number of men in the sample, this difference in ratio is statistically significant ($p = .030$ by a chi square test). Apparently, the tendency for men to go into such careers at a higher rate than women, which has been well established for the general population, occurs for unschoolers as well. The majority of those in STEM in our sample were in some aspect of engineering or computer technology, but the sample also included an archaeologist, field biologist, math and science teacher, intelligence analyst, and four involved in various aspects of medical technology.

In the next and final post on our survey, I will examine the grown unschoolers' overall evaluations of their unschooling experiences. What did they like and not like about being unschooled? What was their social life like? Would they unschool their own children? Are there any who wish they hadn't been unschooled, and, if so, what are their regrets?

11

Survey of Grown Unschoolers IV

What Do Grown Unschoolers Think of Unschooling?

Most were very happy to have been unschooled, but a few were not. Why?

JULY 12, 2014

This is the last in a series of four articles resulting from a survey that Gina Riley and I conducted of 75 adults (age 18 to 49, median age 24) who were unschooled during much or all of what would otherwise have been their K-12 school years. "Unschoolers" do not go to school and, unlike traditional homeschoolers, are not required by their parents or others to do school-like activities at home. They are not presented with a curriculum, required lessons, or a system of academic evaluation. Their parents and others may help in various ways, but unschooled children are in charge of their own educations. Another term for unschooling, favored by some, is "life learning." Unschooled children live their lives, and in the process, they learn. To unschoolers, what we normally think of as the "school years" are not different educationally from other years; people learn all the time. They learn incidentally as they play, work, and converse. They also learn deliberately, to solve real-life problems and to prepare for future steps in life; but, for unschoolers, such deliberate learning is always their own choice, at their own initiative.

In the first article in this series, I described the methods of the survey, presented a breakdown of the respondents based on the last grade of school or homeschool they had completed before unschooling (24 of them had always been unschooled), and presented a statistical summary of the results. In the second article, I elaborate on their experiences with higher education after unschooling. And in the third article, I described the careers they have pursued. In brief, the findings presented in those posts indicate that the grown unschoolers who responded to our survey had no particular difficulty pursuing higher education and careers and often pursued careers that were extensions of passions developed in childhood and involved a high degree of occupational self-direction. Most of the careers chosen were in the creative arts or the STEM category. Now, in this article, I elaborate on the respondents' evaluations of their unschooling experience.

Preference for Unschooling Their Own Children

Perhaps the best indicator of our respondents' feelings about unschooling came in their responses to the ninth and final question in our survey: If you choose to have children, do you think you will choose to unschool them? Why or why not?

One respondent omitted this question. Of the other 74, 50 (67 percent) responded in a way that we interpreted as a clear "yes," indicating that they would definitely unschool their own child, or would unless the child expressed a clear preference for something else or circumstances prevented it. This number includes eight respondents who already had children of school age and were unschooling them. The reasons they gave for preferring to unschool their children are quite similar to the answers they gave (below) to our question about the advantages they experienced in their own unschooling.

Another nineteen (25 percent) responded in a way that we interpreted as "maybe," meaning that they would consider unschooling, but would weigh it against other possibilities, such as a progressive or democratic school. Only five (7 percent) responded in a way that we interpreted as a definite or likely "no." Of these, two were very unhappy about their own unschooling (described later); another felt that unschooling worked well for her but poorly for her younger brother, so she was against unschooling except for highly self-motivated individuals; another preferred democratic schooling (such as a Sudbury school) over unschooling, for the greater sense of community it offered; and a fifth, who was in the military, favored a semi-structured school environment, such as a Montessori school, so the child would learn to follow rules set by others, including ones that seemed arbitrary.

Satisfaction with Social Lives

A common question that homeschoolers and unschoolers alike endure concerns their social lives. An assumption, and a stereotype, is that children who do not attend a school would not make friends, would not learn how to get along with peers, and would grow up socially awkward. At the risk of generating some eye-rolling, we, too, asked about socialization. The sixth question of the survey was: What was your social life like growing up? How did you meet other kids your age? How was your social experience as an unschooler similar to or different from the types of social experiences you have now?

Our coding of responses to this question indicated that 52 (69 percent) of the 75 were clearly happy about their social lives as unschoolers. Of the remaining 23, nine described what we coded as a "poor" social life, and the other 14 expressed mixed feelings. The nine describing a poor social life talked mostly about social isolation—a point to which I'll return later. Those with mixed feelings typically wrote of difficulties finding compatible friends—difficulties that might or might not be attributable to unschooling. (Not everyone in school has an easy time finding compatible friends.)

Most of the respondents appeared to have had no particular difficulty meeting other children and making friends. Forty-one (55 percent) of the 75 wrote that their local homeschooling group was a major source of friendships. Thirty-two (43 percent) stated that organized after-school activities such as dance, theatre, sports, and art classes, provided opportunities to meet others and make friends. Many also mentioned church or religious organizations, community or volunteer associations, and such youth organizations as Boys and Girls Clubs, 4H, and Scouting. Teenagers who took part-time jobs met others through their work. Eight participants made special mention of Not Back to School Camp as a place where they made lasting friendships with other unschoolers, which were maintained through the Internet when camp wasn't in session. Some also stated that their families were very social and involved in the community, so friends were made through family connections.

Even though we didn't ask about age mixing, 51 (68 percent) of the respondents mentioned that interacting with and making friends with people of all ages was a social advantage of not being in school. Many wrote about the special value of friendships with older and younger people. Some pointed out that in the real world, outside of school, people must know how to get along with others of all ages, so, in that sense at least, the social lives of unschoolers (and homeschoolers in general) are more normal than are the age-segregated social lives of children in school.

One 19-year-old woman, who apparently enjoyed (and still enjoys) an especially rich social life, wrote: "I made friends at church or in the neighborhood or through sports or random classes I would take. I made friends at the store, at the post office or at the park. I made friends with people of all walks of life, all ages, all social and economic backgrounds.

Our house was, and still is, a meeting place for many different types of people. We have always had the house where hungry kids came for a meal, where any of my mother's friends or brothers would come for a place to crash when things went awry, or a place for just hiding out for a weekend from all that was bothering them. Some nights we cook for 20 people, others only for our family, so it is never dull. It is a great way to learn about people when you see them in all different situations and all different lights. I have learned what true friends are and have the ability to discern true friendship from passing friendship in most cases. My best friends are a 15-year-old girl who loves to dance and who is crafty, a young man my age who is slowly going blind but who is very driven, and an older woman who is enjoying retirement. It gives me perspectives I don't think I could gain from a group of people only my own age."

An example of a response that we coded as a poor social life was this one, written by a Canadian woman, who was quite happy with other aspects of her unschooling experience: "My social life was not very good, mainly because of our location. It was a very small town with very typical middle-of-nowhere problems. Drinking, drugs, poverty and the like. I realise in retrospect that most of the children who were my neighbours had grown up in a bad situation and didn't know any better, but I didn't understand that at the time and I was miserable. By the time I was a teenager and we had moved to a new province, I found that I just couldn't break into the social groups of the local homeschooling community and, in the end, I wasn't really interested in doing so. My family did things differently, even from an unschooling standpoint, and social experiences usually had an element of culture shock for both parties."

Main Advantages: Freedom and Sense of Personal Responsibility

Question seven of the survey read, "What, for you, were the main advantages of unschooling? Please answer both in terms of how you felt as a child growing up and how you feel now, looking back at your experiences. In your view, how did un-schooling help you in your transition toward adulthood?"

In response to this, the great majority wrote enthusias-tically about the advantages of unschooling. Almost all of them, in various ways, commented on the freedom that un-schooling gave them to find and pursue their own interests and learn in their own ways. Roughly 70 percent also said, in one way or another, that unschooling enabled them to develop as highly self-motivated, self-directed, responsible individuals, who take charge of their own lives. A similar percentage wrote about opportunities for learning they had as unschoolers that would not have been available if they had been in school.

Many also wrote about a seamless transition to adult life. Unschooling is much more like adult life than is school. In this context, a fair number also talked about getting a head start on their careers (discussed in the previous article). They were able to focus and become experts in ways that would not have been possible had they been in school. Some also described how unschooling allowed them to get to know themselves, discover their own passions, and find out how to make their personality work in the world. In this context, several wrote explicitly about learning to value the ways in which they are different from other people and to overcome any fears of being different, or (if always unschooled) about growing up without such fears.

It's interesting to compare these responses to those that parents (mostly mothers) gave to a similar question about the advantages of unschooling that we asked in our previous survey of parents in unschooling families (see The Benefits of Unschooling: Report I from a Large Survey, in this volume). The biggest difference is that 57 percent of the respondents in the parents' survey cited time with family, or increased closeness or harmony, as a major benefit of unschooling, whereas only 24 percent of the grown unschoolers (18 out of the 75) mentioned advantages in this category. This difference is consistent with the view, which I have expressed elsewhere, that children—no matter how much they need and love their parents—are oriented toward moving on, toward adulthood, beyond their family of origin. I think that is one reason why the age-mixed nature of friendships outside of the family was spontaneously mentioned by so many of the respondents to the present survey, and also why they focused so heavily on developing their sense of independence and responsibility. It is interesting, in this regard, that a major complaint of the three who disliked unschooling was that their parents isolated them and prevented them from exploring outside of the family or outside of the insular group with which the family was tied.

As a taste of the ways our respondents described the advantages of unschooling, here are two of the responses to Question seven, somewhat randomly chosen:

A 37-year-old woman who left school after first grade wrote: "The advantages of unschooling for me growing up I felt were (in priority order): 1) being able to sleep when and as long as I needed, 2) having time to do all the things I wanted to do (reading books, building tree forts, knitting, making up plays, riding my bike, playing games, exploring trails in the woods, swimming, baking, making things, etc.), 3) being able to work and make money without school hours getting in the way. Looking back now, I feel all those same things were definitely advantages, more than I knew even at the time! Also, I feel unschooling nurtured my one true talent—completing things. I get stuff done. Unschooling ensured my ability to "think outside the box" as they say, and leaves me now with the ability to make a plan and do it, relishing in negotiating any obstacle and loving having the power to make good things happen. How did unschooling help me in my transition to adulthood? Well, in many ways I started as an adult, responsible for my own thinking and doing, so there was no sudden transition at all."

A 28-year-old woman with no schooling but some curriculum-based homeschooling before unschooling wrote: "As a kid, I felt happy to have so much time out of my day to play and have fun. I could spend more time doing the fun stuff rather than being forced into things I didn't enjoy. As an adult now, I feel I've had the time to explore my own interests and not have activities, knowledge, and ideas forced on me, so instead I grew to enjoy them. For example, I've independently read a lot of classic books since I was young, which I don't think I would have wanted to do if they had been forced on me. . . I've been able to take ideas out of classics that haven't been explained to me (with bias) in some class. In terms of transitioning to adulthood, I've learned to be direct and independent. I never had gender roles forced on me, and don't have a lot of the insecurities and limitations that other women my age have. Because of my knowledge of computer programming, and nerdy interests like Star Trek, I'm very logical and direct. I'm unafraid to say what I mean (although I've learned more tact over the years), and I'm fiercely independent. I don't believe that we're as limited in life as we think."

Main Disadvantage: Dealing with Others' Opinions

Question eight of the survey read, "What, for you, were the main disadvantages of unschooling? Again, please answer both in terms of how you felt as a child growing up and how you feel now. In your view, did unschooling hinder you at all in your transition toward adulthood?"

Twenty-eight of the 75 respondents didn't indicate any disadvantage at all, and most of the rest made it clear that, to them, the disadvantages were minor compared to the advantages. The most frequent category of disadvantage was dealing with other people's opinions—mentioned by 21 (28 percent) of the participants. It's interesting to note that this was also the most frequently mentioned disadvantage in our previous study of unschooling parents, where it was mentioned by 46 percent of the respondents. Dealing with others' opinions seemed to be more distressing to the parents, in the previous study, than to the unschooled children, in the present study. This seems unsurprising, as criticisms and doubts would more often be directed toward parents than toward children, and parents feel responsible for the unschooling decision. A typical comment in this category, in the present study, is the following: "As a kid, I found it endlessly annoying that I had to constantly explain my family's choice to unschool. It wasn't the norm, which was equally exciting and inconvenient."

The next most common disadvantage, mentioned by 16 (21 percent) of the participants, was some degree of social isolation, which came most commonly from the lack of other unschoolers nearby and difficulties of socializing with school children because of their busy schedules and different orientation toward life. For example, one wrote: "The main disadvantage of unschooling for me was that I wasn't in close proximity to other unschoolers after the age of 13. . . My closest friends during my teen years were people I met through NBTSC [Not Back to School Camp] and lived far away." Also included in this category were two or three who complained about lack of dating opportunities.

Only eight (11 percent) mentioned any sort of learning deficit as a disadvantage. Three of these described this as a major disadvantage, and those were the three (described below) who were most unhappy with their unschooling experience. The other five generally indicated that the learning deficit was a minor problem, solved by making up the deficit when they needed to. The most frequently mentioned subject in which they felt deficient, not surprisingly, was math. (As a college professor who taught statistics to social science majors for a number of years, I can attest that many people who studied math for 12 years prior to starting college also complain about, and demonstrate, a deficiency in that subject!)

Why Three Respondents Were Unhappy with Their Unschooling

Of the 75 respondents, only three indicated that the disadvantages, for them, outweighed the advantages. It is instructive to look closely at them, to understand the conditions in which unschooling is not a good idea. In all three cases the mothers were described as in poor mental health and the fathers as uninvolved. In all three cases, the respondents felt socially isolated, ignorant, stigmatized, and "weird" because of their unschooling and their family environment. Two of these respondents attributed the isolation partly to the fundamentalist Christian beliefs of their parents. Here is a brief summary of each case.

One respondent, a 26-year-old woman who grew up in the UK, wrote: "I actively disagree with unschooling because I believe that it is a very easy way for unwell parents to bring their children up without those parents needing to actively participate/integrate into society . . . Because of my mother's poor mental health, she found it difficult making friends and generally disliked attending social events, etc. I think this was the main reason she decided to unschool us." This person went on to say that she felt extremely isolated socially and didn't study anything during her unschooling years. She went on to higher education in fine arts, and a job as an art teacher, not because she was interested in art or enjoyed teaching, but because she didn't feel qualified for anything else. In response to our question about the disadvantages of unschooling, for her, she wrote: "My experience of unschooling was negative in every way. I have been bullied as an adult for being 'weird' and for working in low status, low paid jobs. I have also had difficulty finding long-term boyfriends, as although I'm an attractive and intelligent person, there aren't many people who actively want to date people who have huge chips on their shoulders about the way they were brought up (without formal education)."

The second respondent, a 35-year-old woman, was Christian homeschooled through third grade and then was unschooled, not because of a deliberate decision, but because of her mother's psychological and physical disabilities and consequent inability to manage homeschooling. This person also wrote that her mother kept her out of school "to be able to control the kinds of information we were exposed to, including sex education, science, or health, as well as control the kinds of people we interacted with." She, like the other two, was never presented with a choice about her schooling. She felt deprived of school, not privileged to avoid it. As an adult she has worked mostly at temporary jobs such as cleaning or house painting, but, at the time of the survey, she was enrolled in a bachelor's program in industrial design. In response to our question about the disadvantages of unschooling, she wrote: "Disadvantages would be not having the groundwork of basic knowledge and social skills! I am also uncomfortable with most people and prefer to be alone, which may be from my experience growing up alone and unsupervised, but also might just be my nature, I don't know. As a kid, the main thing was knowing that I was not fitting in anywhere, always being the "weirdos" in the neighborhood, always missing rites of passage and being alone too often. It was a very lonely and isolated life, rather oppressive given the strict religious upbringing. I also feel now that I learned more about religion than I did things that would be of any use to me later in life."

The third respondent, a 29-year-old Ph.D. candidate studying archaeology, wrote that her mother wanted her to have a Christian education, but pulled her out of a Baptist academy in fourth grade because of the mother's conflicts with the staff. The mother intended to homeschool her, using a Christian curriculum, but failed to follow through because of her own psychological depression. In this respondent's words, "Her personal struggles with depression, which led to her inability to function in running a house and supervising my homeschooling activities, was the reason for the switch to unschooling." She wrote further: "In my opinion, I was 'unschooled' simply because my mother could not tolerate the anxiety of having me in public or private school—where non-Christian people could 'negatively influence' me. She needed me at home to do chores and take care of her because she was a non-functional depressed person. She preferred me to have a socially isolated existence from age 9 to 18 than risk a secular education. My father clearly did not want me homeschooled or unschooled, but he never did anything about it and let my mother do as she pleased." Concerning her social life, she wrote: "My 'social' experiences as an unschooler were restricted to inter-actions with my parents, my brother, occasionally more dis-tant family members, and going to the grocery store or doctor when I was sick."

This person was not entirely negative about her unschool-ing. In response to our question about advantages, she wrote: "As an adult looking back, I think being in school while deal-ing with my dysfunctional and abusive parents at home prob-ably would have led me to make some poor social decisions that could have had long-lasting impacts. So, as painful and traumatic as being kept at home in an isolated manner was, I feel it was preferable to the other options. I had a lot of time to myself to think about things. I developed my own secret meditation practice. These habits of self-sufficiency and self-reflectiveness helped me transition toward adulthood, partic-ularly in cutting loose from my mother's controlling grasp." She wrote, in response to an earlier question, "I was also a self-driven learner as an unschooler, and much of my employ-ment now requires self-driven education—whether for my dissertation research or for the development of my teaching pedagogy." She also noted that her interest in archaeology was stimulated in part by her questioning of her parents' belief that the earth was founded 8,000 years ago.

In response to our question about disadvantages of unschooling, she wrote, in part: "As an adult looking back, the main disadvantage was that the social isolation allowed my parents to get away with more abuse and neglect than they otherwise would have. I suffered severe abuse and neglect during the time I was unschooled. Lacking a formal education did chip away at my self-confidence as I transitioned toward adulthood. I carried a nagging sense of unworthiness for quite a while; I still feel permanently damaged in some way, like I am a freak who was kept in a cage and not educated formally. As I prepared to begin formal college education, my unschooling experience hindered me by having failed to provide standard levels of math and science knowledge. I had to tutor myself to pass the GED. I had to tutor myself remedial math and science skills to keep up in introductory-level college courses." I can't refrain from stating here, the obvious: Given her academic success, she must have done a great job of tutoring herself!

It is worth adding that the only other respondent in the whole sample who commented on the role of religion in her upbringing was also very negative about the fundamentalist influence. Her parents became extreme Christian fundamentalists when she was 15. She wrote, "At that time, my role shifted to full-time caretaker for my younger siblings. I was expected to get married and have lots of children rather than having any type of career, so further education was viewed as superfluous in that subculture. . . After my parents became involved with the fundamentalists, we were cut off almost completely from interaction with others outside the tight-knit religious setting. Interactions were mostly centered around child care, chores, and religious meetings with no free time to simply socialize." This person, nevertheless, went on to become a very successful writer and noted that she will unschool her own daughter. She is not against unschooling, but strongly against the social and intellectual isolation that occurred in her home when her parents converted.

A Final Thought

Although the sample is relatively small, the findings of our survey suggest that unschooling can work beautifully if the whole family, including the children, buy into it; if the parents are psychologically healthy and happy; and if the parents are socially connected to the broader world and facilitate their children's involvement with that world. It can even work well when some of these criteria are not fully met. Children growing up unschooled in such environments take control of their own lives and have the support of their families to find and follow their own paths to happiness. But when the dominant parent is truly dysfunctional, or when the family practices a philosophy of isolation from the broader culture rather than integration with it, or when the unschooled child would prefer to go to school, then unschooling can lead to resentment and, quite justifiably, to feelings of abuse and neglect.

Finally, to the participants in the survey, Gina and I say,

THANK YOU for so generously sharing your experiences! This was a lengthy questionnaire to fill out, and many of you wrote long and beautiful essays in response to each question. We have learned much as a result of your willingness to share your experiences.

Printed in the USA
CPSIA information can be obtained
at www.ICGtesting.com
LVHW010526300324
775869LV00005B/1054